SITUATIONAL SENSE

Basic Threat Detection Using Situational Awareness and Common Sense

Matthew Dermody

Situational Sense:
Basic Threat Detection Using Situational Awareness and Common Sense
by Matthew Dermody

© 2019 by Matthew Dermody

ISBN 13: 978-1719969512

Printed in the United States of America

For additional book titles, please visit www.hiddensuccesstactical.com

Other Published Works by Matthew Dermody

Hidden Success: A Comprehensive Guide to Ghillie Suit Construction

Appear to Vanish: Stealth Concepts for Effective Camouflage and Concealment

Gray Man: Camouflage for Crowds, Cities, and Civil Crisis

Hidden in Plain Sight: A Prepper's Guide to Hiding, Discovering, and Scavenging Diversion Safes and Caches

Gray Woman: A Woman's Guide to Gray Man Tactics (eBook)

Conversational Camouflage: Oratory Discretion and Pretexting for Behavioral Concealment

ACKNOWLEDGEMENTS

I would like to thank my friends and colleagues who contributed some of their personal stories and experiences to further explain and put into context the concepts presented within this book.

I also want to thank you, the many readers, who ultimately support my writing career, both individually and collectively. I am humbled by the many that have an interest in the subject matter I present. You have my sincere gratitude.

No acknowledgement section would be complete without the inclusion of my wonderful wife and our twin girls. Their faithful support and encouragement are essential to my writing success. I love you very much.

DEDICATION

This book is dedicated to my father, Harry Dermody, my first teacher on the subjects of self-defense and situational awareness.

TABLE OF CONTENTS

Section Four: EXECUTE

"Life is hard. It's even harder when you're stupid."

- John Wayne

"The most dangerous person is the one who listens, thinks, and observes."

- Bruce Lee

INTRODUCTION

This book is intended to be a starting point for those wishing to increase their observation skills. It also serves seasoned practitioners with an easy to teach and explainable methodology.

There will be those who will find this book to be elementary based upon their own life experience. This book is not necessarily for them. At best, this book would serve them as a refresher to knowledge and skills they already possess. However, those new to the concepts of situational awareness for reasons such as first-time college students, travellers, or those relocating to a new area/region will find the contents beneficial.

What is Situational Sense?

I first introduced the hybrid phrase "situational sense" in my third book, *Gray Man: Camouflage for Crowds, Cities, and Civil Crisis*. Since then, I have reflected on what the phrase entails and thought it beneficial to present it in a book dedicated to exploring the topic in depth. The principles presented within are heavily correlated with the other topics I write about and teach. Because of this previous brief introduction to the subject in *Gray Man*, there are small, selected portions of this work that have appeared in my previously published books. These sections are not intended as filler, but merely to provide clarification, context, or further reinforce the particular subject being addressed.

Situational awareness and common sense are not mutually exclusive; nor are the concepts new. The origins of situational awareness go back to the technical writings supporting the integration of aircraft control and instrumentation displays for commercial aircraft. The term has its modern definition based off of United States Air Force fighter pilots who recognized Situational Awareness to describe the Orient and Observe phases of Boyd's OODA loop.[1]

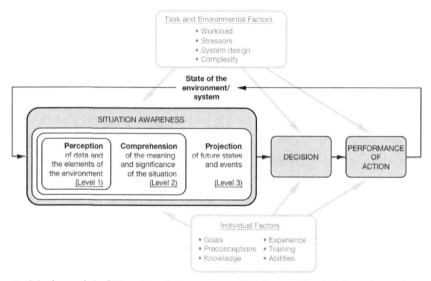

Endsley's model of Situational Awareness. This is a synthesis of versions she has given in several sources, notably Endsley (1995a) and Endsley et al (2000). Drawn by Dr. Peter Lankton, May 2007.[3]

The term common sense goes as far back as the 14th century, meaning originally an internal mental power supposed to unite (reduce to a common perception) the impressions conveyed by the five physical senses (Latin *sensus communis*, Greek *koine aisthesis*). Thus "ordinary understanding, without which one is foolish or insane" (1530s); the meaning "good sense" is from 1726.[2]

In today's modern world, there is such a prevailing mentality for the reliance on technology, governmental services or organizations, to both offer and administer all of our safety needs. We also add the requirement of those same governmental entities to detect and the develop contingencies to eliminate or mitigate any possible threat. These desired outcomes could not be further from our reality. We have become lazy, willfully enslaved by convenience, and bloated with apathy regarding the responsibility for our own safety.

Having the ability and proper skills to fight is good, but it is much better to recognize when the fight is coming. A step further is recognizing it early to prepare or avoid it altogether. It should be noted that being situationally aware and using common sense does not turn you into a battle-hardened warrior or a ruthless, crime-fighting vigilante; despite the implications of the two being significant force multipliers. Awareness is simply recognizing the potential dangers you may be confronted with throughout your life. Based upon this realization, you must determine the amount of resolve and commitment to the training process to ensure that you don't become a victim. In the same manner, possessing situational sense should not morph into an unhealthy display of paranoia.

A majority of the concepts revolving around the subjects of situational awareness, risk mitigation, and crime prevention involve a direct link to the study of human behavior. Despite the attempts of legislators and governmental bodies, they can only attempt to condition behavior. The effectiveness of that conditioning determines our level of conformity and our behavioral choices. We as individuals can only control our behavior, regardless of the temptation or desire to control that of others. Again, we can only attempt to condition favorable behavior.

As a military veteran, I have an over-developed appreciation for acronyms. While there are those who absolutely despise them, I am very comfortable using and remembering acronyms. In fact, in today's fast-paced, tech-driven society, acronyms provide email and texting shortcuts that have been popular before most millenials were even born. Phrases such as FYI (for your information), ASAP (as soon as possible), and DIY (do it yourself) are found all around us. There are many more, but you can see clearly what I mean.

Because of their intended purpose to aid in the recollection of information, I use acronyms in my curriculum and teaching methods. When discussing situational awareness, the acronym I use should unconsciously make students want to become more aware. The word I use is RAPE. It's an unpleasant word. It is violent and abhorrent. It conjures up thoughts of all sorts of horrible imagery that no one ever wants to endure physically and/or emotionally. Rape is such an abuse of power and violation of another's will that its victims struggle with the trauma for years. Some people are traumatized for the rest of their lives. It is my sincere hope that readers and students will remember the acronym rather than having to endure the remembrance of an actual assault bearing its namesake.

Due to its rightfully deserved negative stigma associated with the word rape, it lays the foundation for my approach towards situational awareness. It also serves as a motivation to have more situational awareness and common sense to avoid all assaults and other life-threatening scenarios at all levels of intensity. Not every encounter faced with will start out violent, but it may escalate to violence. Likewise, not every perceived threat will materialize in or follow a specific chronology. The threat may never manifest at all. This book is intended to stimulate you into thinking about and preparing for wise, practical, and tactical ways to respond to crisis.

RAPE is an acronym that stands for REASON, ANALYZE, PREPARE, and EXECUTE. Each word in the acronym contains subcategories, building upon the foundation of my ongoing "S word" alliteration throughout my books and teaching curriculum.

REASON:

Safety
Security
Survival

ANALYZE:

Senses
Scrutiny
Signs
Saboteurs

PREPARE:

Study/Sleuthing
Strategy
Skill-Sets
Systems

EXECUTE:

Street-Smarts
Suppression
Spectators

As a husband and father of two girls, I wish I didn't have to write this book. I wish the evil existing in the world today did not, but it does. I do not possess the power to remove that evil. Nor can I assume to know better than God concerning how to do so. I can only pray, prepare, and practice until confronted with that evil. If it should cross my path, I will protect myself and those in my care. If forced to do so, I'll send those wanting to cause harm to me or those I love, straight to their Maker; or prepare my soul to meet Him myself.

Citations:

[1]https://en.wikipedia.org/wiki/Situation_awareness

[2]https://www.etymonline.com/word/common%20sense

[3]https://en.wikipedia.org/w/index.php?curid=11319693

SECTION ONE

REASON

SAFETY

To paraphrase Looney Tunes creator, Mel Blanc, nobody gets out of life alive. It's a little tongue in cheek, but it's morbidly true. However, that doesn't mean we should look for ways or situations to expedite the inevitable exit from this life with poor choices. Nor should we succumb to defeat as an acceptable outcome when circumstances arise where our personal safety and lives are put at risk at the hands of someone else. Some things we experience we don't get the luxury of choice, but a good portion of what we experience in our lives are the direct result of our choices or how we respond to the situations we must endure.

This doesn't mean we enter into fights and conflicts without assessing every possible means to escape it. As a civilian, you have this ultimate luxury. You are not obligated by law (there are a few exceptions), sense of duty, sworn oath, or professional responsibility to rush into impending danger. Those employed in law enforcement or the military do not have that luxury. Their jobs demand the engagement of the criminal or enemy element as part of their responsibilities and reflect a commitment to the sworn oath to serve, protect, and defend.

Ultimately, you must decide for yourself, regardless of any law, statute, ordinance, act, legislation, or precedent established through case law, that ***you would exercise your God-given rights***,

8

as a human being, to defend yourself and your loved ones when they are in your care or proximity.

Unfortunately, there are those who will seek to infringe upon your rights to life, liberty, and property. Crime, from a legal term, cannot exist without a law decreeing a certain behavior unlawful. Legislators, therefore write, submit, and pass laws, along with the prescribed penalty for its violation. With the unlawful behavior defined and codified, it now justifies the need for that law to be enforced. With the need for enforcement established, people are then hired, trained, and equipped to carry out that enforcement.

Personal safety is often a subjective observation and interpretation. Despite not having all of the facts regarding this photo, many people would feel anxious and threatened if confronted with the situation presented. Photo courtesy of www.pixabay.com.

"Self-defense is a right and not a privilege."

- Louis Awerbuck

You have a natural right to defend yourself. It is the proper role of government to protect and secure those rights. Once another person, group, or corporate entity begins infringing or impeding your rights, then and only then, should the government step in to intervene.

Rights are inherent to all peoples; regardless of color, ethnicity, gender, or creed. Governments attempt to convert rights into privileges to be granted by those in government. Photo courtesy of www.pixabay.com

However, in some forms of government, those in power successfully convince citizens that their rights are merely privileges to be granted. Any rights that benefit or maintain the governmental power are exercised freely without restraint. Those exercising their rights are watched and scrutinized intensely; waiting to impose restrictions or reductions to ensure those rights stay within the beneficial parameters needed for governmental control.

Once those rights potentially threaten the power and status quo of governmental control, those rights are subversively renamed privileges; allowing that government through manipulation and word play to restrict or abolish certain rights. They do this through propaganda, political persuasion, social engineering, virtue signaling, and in extreme cases, totalitarian violence.

If a government insists that self-defense or the tools/methods needed to accomplish it are merely a privilege to be issued under license or bureaucratic regulation, rather than inherit right, this presents that government with a tremendous liability under Common Law. If the people are not permitted to defend themselves, the obligation of protection then falls squarely at the feet of the government and all who serve in some governmental capacity.

"A government big enough to give you everything you want, is a government big enough to take away everything that you have."
- Spurious quote attributed to Thomas Jefferson

That same government must then allow or provide the necessary protection and assume all legal responsibility for its distribution and administration. If it does not, the government should be liable and guilty of one or many of the systematic flaws listed below. Failing to provide protection for its citizens could or would be:

Fiscally irresponsible
Criminally negligent
Improperly trained
Financially underfunded
Inherently biased
Routinely complacent
Commonly absent
Legally liable
Morally repugnant

All of which should make the government 100% responsible when elected representatives and unelected bureaucrats legislate, regulate, and abridge your rights. This, of course, changes the very nature of those rights bestowed by God into the realm of government-granted privileges. Rights are not conditionally granted, only to be revoked later. No matter how narcissistic or self-important government and its officials deem themselves to be, they are not in a position of anything remotely appearing or acting as deity.

Despite the bestowment of rights by God, there are still those who will attempt to take by force or coerce a voluntary surrendering of those rights. Think about the name Bill of Rights for a second. When you hand someone a bill, you're legally invoking a demand for payment and the recipient is legally obligated to pay. The Bill of Rights isn't some nice list of rights we'd like to have someday. It's a demand *by the people* placed on the government stating, "You WILL secure and protect these rights for every person and are legally obliged to do so." Elected officials and those charged with the enforcement of our nation's laws swear an oath to uphold the Constitution. You'd better make sure they do it.

The gritty, undeniable <u>FACTS</u> about self-defense...

1. **YOU** are ultimately responsible for your safety.

2. The police only have a **GENERAL** obligation to protect and serve.

3. Police response times are several **MINUTES** when **SECONDS** count.

4. Escape, whenever possible, is **NOT** cowardice.

5. Fighting is always the **LAST** resort.

YOU are ultimately responsible for your safety.

You, not your partner, not your friends, not politicians, not lawyers, not bystanders, not security officers, not even the police, are responsible for your safety and well-being. Duty of Care or Good Samaritan legislation can only do so much; and only if any of the above-mentioned people are present during the exact moment of your need and request for assistance.

This principle cannot be reiterated enough. You are your strongest defense, loudest advocate, and greatest beneficiary of all that you do in the name of your self-interest. Photo courtesy of www.pixabay.com.

Unless you have the financial means to hire close personal protection or bodyguards, you must be willing to act decisively and prudently on your own behalf in regards to your safety. The alternative is the willingness to accept the consequences if you choose not to act. It is that simple.

Your own opinions on the legislative restrictions of firearms, knives, tasers, and pepper spray may vary or align with other Americans. Regardless of your personal opinion on defensive weapons, you can be certain that criminals, by their very nature and definition, have neither regard for legislation, nor its enforcement. The consequences are often not a strong enough deterrent, either.

The government and police only have a GENERAL obligation to protect and serve.

Despite the slogan affixed to patrol vehicles or promoted on government websites, there is a big difference between *your* safety and *public* safety. Police operate under the umbrella of what is regarded as the public's best interest, even if an individual suffers in order to fulfill that mandate. The fact that you exist within that sphere of "the public" doesn't necessarily entitle you to any public protections.

"To Serve and Protect" is a common slogan found on patrol vehicles. In reality, the phrase provides nothing more than lip service and a false sense of security. Photo courtesy of www.pixabay.com.

Police are not in the protection business, they enforce law. The only time protection is offered is during an attempt to enforce law. If officers respond to a call out where the commission of a crime is still active and ongoing, they are obligated to use whatever force is reasonable and necessary to end the commission of that crime. Even then, that obligation is still subject to their discretion in regards to officer safety.   Further cementing this statement is the recent upholding of several court rulings that directly reflect this, and in some rulings, use this statement verbatim.[1]

Police response times are several MINUTES when SECONDS count.

Response times by police and emergency services can vary drastically. There are many factors contributing to potentially long response times in an emergency. As such, you must prepare and proceed as if assistance is *not coming*. As taxpayers in a generally civil society, we expect those services to be there when we need them. After all, we are funding those services with our tax dollars. However, we often discover or become aware of misuse or misappropriation of tax dollars. This neither conveys any confidence in a government's ability to spend revenue wisely, nor does it solve any of the societal woes regarding crime.

Society can hardly expect police officers to provide adequate law enforcement services without a salary.   Not only is law enforcement a potentially dangerous occupation, it is often a thankless one. Add to this the alarming trend that fewer people want to enter law enforcement as a career.[2] Police departments in some regions of the country have begun to lower requirements and training standards in order to meet the urgent need for officers on the street.

A large-scale disaster or massive civil unrest may see police officers choosing to abandon others for the sake of caring for and protecting their own families.[3]   This happened in New Orleans in 2005 with hurricane Katrina. With close to 125 billion dollars worth of damage and a death toll of over 1,800 people, one can clearly see the results of government efficiency.[4]   While it's easy to blame officials and law enforcement for many of the unnecessary deaths, it's not difficult to understand why.

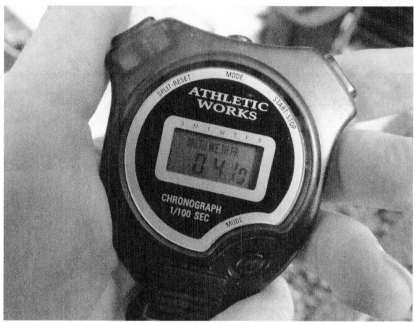

Violent attacks are frequently over long before the police arrive to intervene and protect you. Photo courtesy of www.pixabay.com.

Escape, whenever possible, is NOT cowardice.

Running away may not seem brave or heroic, but it is often the best alternative before the last resort of physical conflict. Because running is a viable defense mechanism, criminals often targets individuals who cannot run (i.e. the elderly or obese) or those whom they reasonably feel they can outrun or catch. Footwear is a major consideration for criminals choosing their potential victims. Australia is known for its flip-flop/thong foot attire or no footwear at all.[5] Both choices can greatly impede one's ability to run quickly, safely, and effectively. High-heeled shoes should be replaced with more comfortable and practical shoes in the event of walking into areas or situations where the need to move rapidly may occur. Even worse, is being barefoot. Most people in developed countries have such a reliance on footwear that they cannot run fast or without impediment when barefoot. I'm reminded of the movie *Die Hard*, where Bruce Willis' character had taken off his shoes prior to the terrorist strike and had to fight a slew of terrorists; running through a building without shoes. The terrorists even tried to take advantage of his mistake by shooting up glass; creating a floor full of razor sharp confetti. The result was messy and bloody.

"Ultimate victory is in avoiding the fight."

- Sun Tzu

Running or walking away from a potential threat may not seem very heroic or courageous; but when facing multiple attackers, running is often the safest option. Photo courtesy of www.pixabay.com.

Fighting is always the LAST resort.

When speaking about violence, Martin Luther King, Jr. said, "It doesn't solve anything." Philosophically speaking, he was right about violence begetting more violence. However, in matters of self-defense, violence doesn't solve anything, except when it does. Violent, aggressive behavior and fighting is ugly. It is only flashy and choreographed in the movies. Opponents do not intentionally trade punches back and forth in some kind of ritualistic show of chivalry and civility. Likewise, multiple attackers don't politely take turns, allowing you to square off with one attacker at a time. They attack like a pack of hyenas simultaneously.

The barrage continues until the other submits, succumbs to injury, or is able to mount a successful counter-attack. Adrenaline can only stave off pain receptors for a limited time. After the adrenaline wears off, the body immediately begins to notify the brain of sustained injury. Movies such as John Wick depict an unnatural resilience and ability to function despite repeated injuries, which under realistic circumstances; most people would simply collapse from the physical trauma and prolonged exertion.

Fighting and fighting systems have been around since the dawn of human history. There is nothing new under the sun in this regard. Don't be sucked into fad fighting systems; rather, choose a system that compliments your abilities. Photo courtesy of www.pixabay.com

This brings us to the first truth in fighting. You will be hit. You will probably sustain some type of injury as a direct result. Unless you are the *initial* aggressor, which you shouldn't be from a legal or self-defense standpoint, you must allow your attacker to make the first move. This *does not* mean you allow them to be successful or land punches and strikes upon you. It simply means that in doing so; you can legally portray yourself as the initial victim of an unlawful assault. This also means that you cannot provoke, either verbally or through body language, an invitation to a physical altercation.

"The world is a dangerous place to live; not because of the people who are evil, but because of the people who don't do anything about it."

- Albert Einstein

This is a view no one ever wants to experience. You may never find yourself in this type of situation. You must train and prepare as if you will encounter threats such as this and then act decisively. Photo courtesy of www.pixabay.com

When all other options have been exhausted, fighting back is your best option. Petty criminals who thrive upon opportunity don't like the odds stacked against them. They want to get what they want fast and get away faster. Conflict or resistance offered up by their intended victim prevents them from achieving their main goals: Tangible goods and escape.

The truth is; anyone is a potential target...

Most people don't want to get dirty or bloodied. It's even safer to assume that most people don't want to die and subsequently buried. Both of the statements relate to dirt and soil. Therefore, SOILED is a good acronym to describe how criminals target potential victims and the desired status of their prey.

Criminals want you...

S - Solitary or Separated
O - Ostracized and Oblivious
I - Isolated and Insufficiently prepared
L - Lonely and Lacking
E - Excluded and Empty-handed
D - Defenseless or Dead

Don't give criminals or tyrants what they want. Criminals choose targets that are by themselves or have distanced themselves from others in their group. Perpetrators want targets that are clueless about their criminal intentions and even more clueless when it comes to responding to their demands. Lastly, criminals want targets that don't know how to respond assertively and decisively to a threat; lacking the tools, the means, and the will to fight back. Don't give them what they want. Become a hard target rather than an easy prey.

Citations:

[1]*DeShaney v. Winnebago County*, 489 U.S. 189 (1989), *Town of Castle Rock v. Gonzales*, 545 U.S. 748 (2005), *Warren v. District of Columbia, 444 A. 2d 1 - DC: Court of Appeals 1981*

[2]https://www.washingtonpost.com/crime-law/2018/12/04/who-wants-be-police-officer-job-applications-plummet-most-us-departments/

[3]https://www.nytimes.com/2005/09/04/us/nationalspecial/law-officers-overwhelmed-are-quitting-the-force.html

[4]https://en.wikipedia.org/wiki/Hurricane_Katrina

[5]https://www.canberratimes.com.au/story/6209561/all-hail-the-thong-australias-shoe-of-choice/

SECURITY

"We are doing everything we can" is the most impotent, dispassionate lullaby ever sung by politicians, city officials, and law enforcement. The word "everything" is an interchangeable word in their vocabulary for something and anything. As long as they can articulate and prove that they have attempted something or anything, those claiming that nothing was done are refuted and discredited. Regardless of how poorly executed, planned, or financed that something or anything is; they feel justified in their statement. Those claiming they didn't do enough will be marginalized with false empathy and feeble excuses, with victims rarely taking any solace, comfort, or healing in their words.

It's no secret that there simply are not enough law enforcement personnel on the streets today to prevent crime effectively. Most police work does one of two things. It potentially deters the commission of crime or it investigates crimes after the fact. Even police intervention during the commission of some crimes doesn't prevent the initial attack, but merely stops the continuance.

So the question then becomes, are we, as individuals, doing everything we can to protect our loved ones and ourselves? For most of society, that answer is no. We tend to live in our little bubbles of general politeness and civility. But what happens when someone comes along and intentionally, maliciously pokes a hole in our bubble? How do we respond?

The human mind and body are equipped to respond with physical and mental defense mechanisms for coping with everything from anxiety to zoophobia. In a crisis, situations and circumstances can change rapidly, providing little time and opportunity to respond effectively in the formulation and execution of a workable plan. Therefore, the best solution is to acknowledge the potential for a crisis, keep vigilant watch for crisis indicators, and have a plan prior to a crisis or confrontation.

Modified Kubler-Ross Change Curve for Change Management:

Developed by the Swiss psychiatrist Elisabeth Kubler-Ross, this change management model explains how people experiencing grief undergo five basic emotions: denial, anger, bargaining, depression, and finally, acceptance. Other modified models add two more stages: shock and testing. In those models, shock appears prior to the onset of denial and testing manifesting between the depression and acceptance stages. These are not exclusive to the grieving process and can be applied to many types of crisis. Many of the potential life-threatening encounters we could face fall into one of the Kubler-Ross reaction categories. They can also transition from one to another rather quickly.

Shock - Initial paralysis at hearing/seeing crisis
Denial - Attempts to avoid the inevitable crisis
Anger - Displays of penned-up emotion
Bargaining - Vainly seeking alternatives to escape
Depression - Realization of the inevitable crisis
Testing - Seeking realistic solutions to the crisis
Acceptance - Finding a way forward regardless of crisis outcome[1]

Another conceptual model used to ascribe and justify behavior patterns is Maslow's Hierarchy of Needs. This model is often diagramed as a pyramid with the larger biological and physiological needs serving as the foundation for all other needs to be built upon.

According to Abraham Maslow's Hierarchy of Needs, safety is the second foundational need just after biological and physiological needs. We often forego the upper levels of Maslow's triangle in order to assure the foundations or baseline of existence. For example, we may put our personal safety or reputation at risk to fulfill biological needs such as food and water. This also means that others will inevitably do the same. When people cannot meet their basic needs, they'll turn to whatever behavior is necessary to obtain or meet those needs.

Maslow's Hierarchy of Needs:

Biological and Physiological needs - Basic life needs; air, food, drink, shelter, warmth, sex, sleep, etc.

Safety needs - Protection, security, order, law, limits, stability, etc.

Belongingness and Love needs - Family, affection, relationships, work groups, etc.

Esteem needs - Achievement, status, responsibility, reputation.

Cognitive needs - Knowledge, meaning, self-awareness.

Aesthetic needs - Beauty, balance, form, etc.

Self-actualization - Personal growth, self-fulfillment.

Transcendence - Helping others to self-actualize.[2]

YOUR HOME IS YOUR CASTLE...

The old saying, "Your home is your castle" is great starting point for your personal security. You should feel the safest in your home. Regardless of the neighborhood or other outside factors, no one should be able to come through your front door without your permission or invitation.

Not only is a dog a great pet and companion in terms of Maslow's Hierarchy of Needs, it is also a great security asset. Photo courtesy of www.pixabay.com

You can visit almost any police website and be sure to find a list of tips to help secure your home and make it less attractive to criminals. In the past, home security was only affordable to the upper middle-classes and higher in the socio-economic structure of American society. However, technology has advanced in such a way where more and more people can afford it or have decided it to be a much higher priority than in the past. Home security systems are connected to Smartphones through a variety of apps and monitoring services. You can control lights, remotely arm and disarm intrusion sensors, monitor temperature, turn on and off appliances, all from apps on your phone.

In the website resources section listed in the back of the book, you'll find a few websites listed with helpful hints and tips to help secure your home.

THE SIX LEVELS OF PERSONAL SECURITY

Just like any well-conceived security strategy, I teach a six-layered model of personal security. They are Sanctum, Structures/Sites, Stores, Sanctuaries/Schools, Stadiums, and Streets. Each level is more populated, thus increasing the potential for crisis. In the post 9/11 world, the more populated an area or event is, the greater the potential threat of becoming a target for terrorism is.

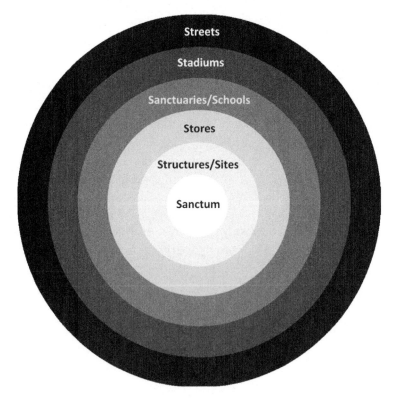

The Six Levels of Personal Security. Graphic by author.

Sanctum - Your home should be your sanctum; your safest place where you can rest. Webster's dictionary defines sanctum as a place free from intrusion.[3] To the degree you fortify your home with the various privacy and anti-intrusion theft measures available to you, will add to how much you "feel" safe. With the exception of determined and targeted criminal behavior against you or the serving and lawful execution of a warrant, you have the final say as to who may cross the threshold into your house.

Whether you live in a single dwelling home or an apartment complex, make sure it is well lit, well maintained, and if possible, has controlled entry gates.
Photo courtesy www.pixabay.com

Structures/Sites - These are your places of employment outside your home. On average, they tend to be larger than your home, but smaller than stores and shopping centers.

Stores - Stores and local shops are the next progression within our daily activities.

Sanctuaries/Schools - Schools and places of worship have either controlled access based on enrollment, membership, or denominational belief.

Stadiums - Stadiums contain larger venues with attendance populations reaching the tens of thousands depending on the size of the stadium and the popularity of the hosted event. Typical examples are convention centers, casinos, outdoor concert venues, etc. Access into the facility is granted and controlled by ticket purchases or authorized/legitimate access through a third party service, such as a food vendor, security, or custodial service. This category also includes large transportation hubs such as airports, train stations, bus terminals, etc. and is the bridge into the street level.

Streets - The largest group listed is the streets. This is where there is the greatest number of threats that most people will encounter those potential threats. The threats are also varied as they can come in pedestrian, vehicular, and structural forms.

MORE PEOPLE, MORE POTENTIAL CONFLICT...

As each ring stretches outward, the population grows as the ability to limit or restrict access decreases. The only place where you have the final word regarding access and population is within the walls of your home. An average home capacity is based on 1 - 6 regular occupants, with the ability to accommodate up to a dozen more, depending on the event, i.e. visits from family members or entertaining friends.

Your workplace attendance can vary from 5-100+ employees, depending on the size of the employer and the type of business being conducted.

Places of worship and schools can have attendance ranging from 100 - 1000+ students or parishioners. Colleges and universities can vary in attendance/population levels from 1000s of students to a couple of ten thousand students. There are also very large church congregations that can exceed the 5,000 attendees mark on any given Sunday.

Stadiums can easily reach capacities from 1,000 - 40,000+ attendees, depending on the event. Security at these large venues can quickly become a logistical nightmare, especially if a rapid evacuation is necessary. The number of potential bottlenecks almost guarantees injuries among fleeing spectators.

Terror groups target this ring often because of the concentration of people. A small, but significant attack is launched to frighten and create panic. As people hastily exit, a secondary attack is set off to injure, maim, or kill as many people as possible, using exits and other means of egress as funnels for victims to run. With high profile people, entertainers, and politicians attending high-visibility events or passing through an airport, you can understand why terrorists target such places.

When you combine both the pedestrian and vehicle traffic on the streets, you can see the increased risk to personal security. Depending on the city, time of day and time of year, there can be 10,000 - 1,000,000+ people all trying to move around. Granted, not all will be in the same vicinity, heading in the same direction, or to the same location. However, the abundance of people will affect how and where you can move.

Your safety and security are ultimately up to you. You decide how vigilant you're going to be and to what degree you're willing to rely on other people to rescue you. What price will you place on your security and that of your loved ones?

Citations:

[1] https://www.cleverism.com/understanding-kubler-ross-change-curve/

[2] https://www.explorepsychology.com/maslows-hierarchy-of-needs/

[3]   https://www.merriam-webster.com/dictionary/sanctum

SURVIVAL

Humans are survivors. It is hard-wired into our DNA. Our ability to think, reason, and invent are all deeply rooted in our ingrained instinct to do whatever is necessary to live and survive.

Often this image comes to mind when people are asked about what survival is. Survival is more than emergency response or sustained lifestyle away from civilization. Photo courtesy of www.pixabay.com.

The first thing making survival possible is knowledge, followed closely by having access and use of tools. This is reinforced by the Boy Scout motto, "Be Prepared." For example, primitive man sees an animal that will provide something he

31

needs in order to survive. He grabs a stone and throws it at the animal, striking and stunning it. He approaches the animal, only to have it jump up suddenly and gorge him to death. Another man observes what has happened and decides to use a bigger rock and a pointed stick as an additional weapon. He learns from the other man's mistake, utilizing the knowledge he obtained through observation and successfully kills the animal for his survival. Knowledge and tools, tools and knowledge; they go hand and hand in procurement, carry, and application.

THE IMPORTANCE OF THE EDC KIT...

Besides the importance of carrying such a kit, it is important to understand both the advantages and limitations of each item within your kit. Furthermore, your EDC kit may be different from one carried by someone else. A certain piece of gear may not be needed in your kit, but critical in another's.

In order to carry most items conveniently, the items must be pocket-sized. For example, while having a large, D-size battery Mag-Lite would provide ample lighting in any situation and serve as an emergency defense baton. However, carrying one on your person is quite impractical and cumbersome.

Sometimes the best items are also keychain-sized. This does affect some of the durability and functionality of some items. However, the key is for the item to help you manage a sudden or emerging crisis, not sustain you for several days or weeks. This doesn't mean the item(s) can't or won't last longer. For instance, a multi-tool may help you tighten or loosen screws for whatever reason. You won't wear out the tip on that particular tool, but, for most routine jobs, a full-size screwdriver is the better choice. Purpose-based ergonomic design and convenience will easily outperform a pocket-sized all-in-one tool design.

EDC (Every Day Carry) Kit - Internet searches on websites like Pinterest and Instagram can provide a clear overview of the myriad of items one could/should carry every day. Some items are viewed as universal and some are viewed as personal preference carry. Carry location isn't as important as having the items available on your person when needed. For example, a small liquid compass may get lost within a pouch or even fall out unnoticed. I wear mine on my watchband instead of carrying it loose in a pocket or on a paracord bracelet. An executive may not need to carry a pen in his EDC kit, because he already has a pen in his shirt pocket.[1]

Personal preference dictates what you want and/or need for EDC. Photo by author.

"Better to have, and not need, than to need, and not have."

- Franz Kafka

It's also important to recognize the word "kit" is a bit of a misnomer. The contents of your EDC may not be contained in a single bag, compartment, or pocket. They are more likely distributed to several pockets or small pouches. This is done for a couple of reasons. First, it spreads out and balances the weight of the items across the body. Second, it makes items more practically accessible and deployable. Third, it reduces bulges or "printing" of certain items.

The following is a list of common EDC items:[1]

Folding Knife - A good majority of people, especially men, tend to carry a folding pocketknife of some variation on their person. It's a good idea to carry a secondary one inside your EDC kit.

Flashlight - A small LED, push-button flashlight is all that is necessary. It really depends on how bulky you want your fully loaded EDC kit to be. A larger hand-held light with a crenulated bezel makes an efficient, improvised impact weapon.

First-aid/Trauma Kit - Carrying a small first-aid/trauma kit is important, especially if you carry a concealed firearm. You should be adequately trained or knowledgeable to treat minor to moderate injuries. Major wound care demands training that is more intensive or may require certification, but having the means to render aid until first responders arrive is crucial.

Prescription Medications - If you take doctor prescribed medications, it's a good idea to have a few spares located within a waterproof vial. Label it with the drug name(s) and dosage, if necessary.

Pen and Small Notebook - As a writer, I find having a pen and paper available to be invaluable for jotting down ideas and notes. Having these items available to you can make documenting important observations, dates and times of specific events, contact names, phone numbers, and addresses. Relying on your memory as times goes by after an event often results in information being left out. Sometimes that information is crucial to an investigation or court proceeding.

Wristwatch - A watch obviously informs the wearer of the time and is less conspicuous and inherently distracting to look at compared to a cell phone. The watch should be rugged and non-reflective (as much as possible). Expensive, high-end watches should be avoided, just as jewelry make nice targets for thieves.

Whistle - A small whistle is a loud, distinct way to either request assistance, ward off an attacker, or notify others of danger. Some whistles are even integrated into plastic buckles on the ever-popular paracord bracelets.

Cell Phone - Despite the drawbacks to the dependency on technology, a cell phone or smart phone is still useful. It can provide you with an emergency device for calling police or navigating your way through an unfamiliar city. The cell phone may be able to replace certain items such as a compass, flashlight, wristwatch, and notepad with an appropriate app. It depends on how technology dependent you want to be with your EDC. Remember, it is an electronic device requiring a power supply and a network to function at its greatest potential. Otherwise, it's an over-priced paperweight.

SERE Kit - I carry a small pocket sized SERE kit contained within a small plastic case originally designed to hold a Compact Flash storage device. Some of the items contained within are two cyalume mini chem-sticks (one red, one green), a ceramic razor blade, a polymer handcuff key, two metal paper clips (for improvised lock picks), a 1-inch IR (infrared) patch, and a key fob LED light. The case is held shut with two Ranger Bands cut from a bicycle tire tube. The overall size of the kit is 1.75" x 2" x .375" and fits comfortably and is relatively unnoticeable in my front pants pocket. When packed tightly, the contents don't rattle.

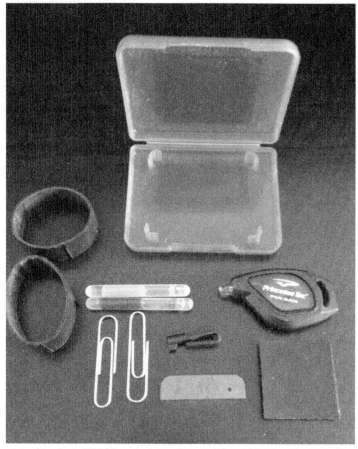

Items contained in a basic SERE kit can assist you in escape from abductions, hostage situations, or unlawful detainment. Photo by author.

Multi-Tool - A compact, folding tool with multiple functions are necessary for small, quick repairs. While not all included tools are as effective or functional as often advertised, a multi-tool works in a pinch without having to carry a hefty toolbox.

Disposable Lighter - A cigarette lighter is useful regardless of whether or not you smoke. This probably is a Cold War espionage holdover due to the fact that many people smoked during the 1950s and 60s and was a relevant icebreaker question. It's also a quick fire-starting method and emergency light source.

Compass - A liquid filled dial compass can give the user a quick bearing either when the sun is not visible in the sky because of overcast conditions or structures blocking it.

Concealed Carry Firearm - Personal preference will dictate where you carry most of your personal defense weapons. Carry placement is a debate almost as heated and ongoing as the 9mm vs. .45 arguments. My opinion reflects how I want to integrate the Gray Man concept: Nothing showing, nothing sticking out. Some readers will agree with my stance, some won't. My carry position is not the only option or the correct option, but it is the best option for me. Simply put, your carry position has to work for you; meaning you are able to present the weapon when needed, both swiftly and safely.

In addition, you should also carry at least one spare magazine or reload for each concealed carry firearm you have in your possession. Some people choose to carry more. A workable compromise must be reached between personal comfort and a person's determination of an appropriate and portable ammunition reserve.

Other Weapons - It should be understood, but for the sake of legal clarity, let me reiterate the importance of carrying ANY weapon in accordance with federal, state, and local laws. Before traveling, research the carry laws in other states and when traveling internationally. Choose weapons that are legal to carry. In extreme cases of civil crisis, laws and the enforcement of those laws may become irrelevant. Follow your convictions and plan accordingly to accept contingencies and consequences based upon your carry decisions. Please refer to Chapter 11, the chapter on *Systems* for a list of improvised carry weapons.

Optional Carry Gear - The addition of extra gear can be a nice insurance policy. Extra gear is not necessary, but neither is it forbidden. It becomes an issue of personal preference. The main purpose is to have items that you may potentially need without having to carry large packs or have bulging pockets resembling the over-stuffed cheeks of a chipmunk. Too many objects in one pocket can make it harder to rapidly or effectively deploy items when they are needed.

Dump Wallet - Sometimes the best thing in a confrontation is to cut your losses and run. A dump wallet can help accomplish this. A dump wallet is a secondary wallet containing fake credit cards, some generic photos of people not related or known to you, and maybe some low denomination paper currency.[2] The opportunistic thug doesn't want a conflict escalation any more than his potential victim. This isn't always the case, but criminals know the more physical harm they inflict upon their victim, the more likely the police will intensify their search for the culprit.

Promotional insert cards from credit lenders are great for stuffing in a dump wallet. Some look legitimate and contain no personal information. RFID sleeves can help hide the fake cards. Photo by author.

Unfortunately, there are no hard and fast rules regarding the handling of violent situations when presented to individuals. It is best to throw a dump wallet away from you and your desired direction of travel. This gives you the opportunity to run and the criminal gets his consolation prize. Tossing the dump wallet to the ground may offer enough of a distraction to escape or launch a counter-attack to stop the threat. Avoid just handling over the dump wallet, allowing the thug to inspect its contents before he grants you permission to leave. Throw it and run.

Despite the earlier advice shown in the previous photo, some of the promotional credit cards do not look realistic enough to fool people. As some criminals know about the use of dump wallets, if the cards look like fakes, they may demand your real wallet. You can use expired credit and debit cards **IF** you do the following:

1.   Ensure the card is expired/deactivated and you are in possession of its activated replacement.

2. Gently sand the embossed name and signature area so your name does not appear or is now unreadable. Most credit cards placed inside of wallets only show the upper portion of the card and won't reveal the redacted area. This will add the look of authenticity to your dump wallet.

3. Degaussing the card ensures none of the stored information is accessible or retrievable should a thief attempt to access the card.[3] Degaussing can be accomplished with a couple of rare earth magnets and passing the card's magnetic strip through them.

NOTE: Take advantage of RFID card sleeves by placing expired or low-value gift cards in them. RFID sleeves give an added validity to the card contained as being authentic. Be sure to record the card numbers along with logins to check the balances after a theft. Criminals will sometimes try to redeem them for cash or attempt to purchase items for the issuing store. The police can sometimes identify and track down the suspect through the transactions.

PACK OR HERD: SURVIVAL OF THE MOST PREPARED

Survival isn't reserved for the fittest. Despite Herbert Spencer's coining of the phrase, "survival of the fittest" it simply means reproductive success as a way of continuing the existence of a species. Charles Darwin went on to borrow the phrase in his work, *On the Origin of Species*.[4] Throughout history, we have seen through the focused lens of society, those who survive regardless of how fit or unfit an individual is. As Spencer clearly discussed, it has nothing to do with genetic fitness, mental fitness, or physical fitness. That isn't to say those factors don't influence a person's chances of survival. However, some people manage to survive, even when the odds are stacked against them.

The choice is yours to develop and maintain a predatory pack mentality or a prey herd mentality. Photos courtesy of www.pixabay.com

Survival can be explained with two extreme animalistic mindsets. You can have a herd mentality, which is one of succumbing to the role of prey. This mentality is often frowned upon by free-thinking, self-reliant individuals as this mindset is often characterized as conformist, docile, and pacifist.

The opposite is choosing to operate with a pack mentality, where you position yourself as a predator; taking advantage of the young, the weak, the old, and the sick. This mentality is characterized as aggressive, volatile, and unpredictable.

The animal world has plenty of examples of both prey and predator. Prey animals rely on their ability to run away, strength in numbers, and sacrificing one another for sake of the rest. Predators rely on patient stalking and sudden attacks. In some cases, strength in numbers manifests itself with multiple predators cutting off all escape routes and overpowering the isolated prey.

In order to avoid the extremes of either mentality, we must consciously choose to avoid herding ourselves amongst the flock of potential victims and distance ourselves from the temptation to become the vigilante and inadvertently turn into the very predatory monster we despise.

I like to think of a bear as a relevant analogy for a survival mindset. Bears are definitely not social creatures like canines and primates, but they can interact in relative peace with other bears. If you see more than one together, it's usually a sow with cubs. The sow only becomes aggressive if she feels the cubs are in danger. Bears are given a wide berth by other predators and don't go about looking to get into conflict. They are shy and often choose to shuffle off rather than look for conflict. They are not malicious or ferocious, but aggressive when threatened or provoked. Bears are not territorial, but do have a comfort zone when it comes to personal space.[5]

Despite a number of positive correlations to bears and the attitudes towards survival and situational sense we should adopt, there are drawbacks that will be discussed throughout this book. Specifically, bears are not always aware of their surroundings.

However, before I get too far along on a tangent, it is for this very reason regarding awareness, that I have dedicated myself to further study and to share what I know.

Citations:

[1]Direct quotes from the EDC section of Chapter 11, titled Supplies from the previously published, *Gray Man: Camouflage for Crowds, Cities, and Civil Crisis.*

[2]http://www.itstactical.com/intellicom/diy/deceive-a-mugger-with-a-diy-decoy-wallet/

[3]https://www.protondata.com/blog/data-security/what-is-degaussing/

[4]https://en.wikipedia.org/wiki/Survival_of_the_fittest

[5] http://www.bearsmart.com/about-bears/behaviour/

SECTION TWO

ANALYZE

SENSES

Our senses help us receive information from the world around us. They are crucial to the concept of danger avoidance and to the detection of threats. Any distraction, degradation, or disability in any of the five senses puts us at greater risk for danger. Danger can vary from minor injury to great peril or even death.

In addition to our senses, our cognitive ability to assess the received information and compare it with attained knowledge, instinct, or experience is critical to our day-to-day survival. Imagine what it would be like if it was impossible to remember our bodies auto-response to certain stimuli. How many times would we burn ourselves on the stove? How many peoples' lives are cut short for failing to look both directions before crossing the street? These are but two examples showing the importance of having the ability to recall information regarding potential danger.

The Five Senses:

Most texts regarding the five senses often list them as Vision, Hearing, Smell, Touch, and Taste. In every book I've published which mentions them specifically, I've always assigned an S word for each of the five senses for the sake of uniformity.

It's merely done for presentations and lectures, not to set a new standard as to how they are classified or discussed elsewhere. My list consists of the following:

Sight
Sound
Smell
Skin
Sublingual

Your senses are going to receive and interpret stimuli that ultimately influence your response to danger. Many times, there are warning signs or indicators of something not being right prior to an attack. When those signs are absent or concealed, it sets up an ambush situation. These are the most dangerous. Unless you prepare your responses in advance and expect the possibility of an ambush, you are likely to be caught unprepared and succumb to it.

There are many who believe in what is commonly referred to as a sixth sense. Some call this phenomenon clairvoyance, premonition, intuition, gut feeling, discernment, or a hunch. Regardless of the terminology, its usefulness cannot be overstated. How many times have you second-guessed yourself, only to find out your initial thought concerning the course of action to take was the correct choice? Consider when the hair on the back of your neck stands up. Your skin is the largest sensory organ. When your hair stands up on your neck, it acts like a huge antenna, sending a message to your brain that something isn't right.

EYES IN THE BACK OF YOUR HEAD...

This is an old saying that countless children have heard from their parents. But, what does it mean? It means that we do not have to turn our heads physically to point our eyes at what we wish to observe.

Using the reflection in flat surfaces is like using a rear view mirror while you walk. This keeps you from having to look over your shoulder constantly. Photo courtesy of www.pixabay.com

Any flat, smooth surface, regardless of any horizontal, vertical, or diagonal orientation can become a reflector or mirror. The level of clarity and detail are affected by the surface material, lighting, angle, and cleanliness, but many structures that don't have eyes can become our eyes. Using your Smartphone as a reflective surface is the only time I can recommend that your phone be in your hand. Pretending to take a selfie allows you to angle the screen to observe persons or things behind you.

Another area from which danger and attacks can come is from an elevated position. These attacks can occur in either wilderness or urban environments. Combat and tactical trackers make it a point to look up, especially when tracking enemy troops or fugitives. Our tendency is focus our attention on the ground rather than trees and other elevated structures because that's where a majority of threats manifest. Failing to look up can leave you susceptible to ambush or detect some other danger. For tactical operatives and law enforcement, it can mean failing to acquire and apprehend a fugitive.

This brings the introduction of a couple of simple acronyms regarding observation techniques. Our eyes are our primary threat detectors. In instances where accidents/fatalities occur, most often the victim didn't see or failed to see the threat coming.

PRECIOUS LIKE GOLD AND SILVER...

Just as gold and silver are regarded as precious, your life, too, is precious; both to you and the people who love and care about you. There are other people, like family and friends, whom you value and desire that no harm come to them.

GOLD is an acronym standing for *Glance, Observe, Look, and Decide.* While the first three words involve the action of acquiring visual input, the duration and intent of each word is different. At each stage, a decision is made to either disregard the input as non-threatening or regard the viewed behavior as worthy of further scrutiny.

Glance - This is just a brief, initial check, but is often the result of some stimuli that catches our attention. It could be color, movement, or loud noise that activates our sensory organs into threat detection mode.

Observe - This stage warrants more scrutiny and attempts to determine intention and motive of the watched individual. Following with the eyes and staring are common, trying to gather enough information to proceed to the next step of risk assessment.

Look - This stage begins searching for exits routes or pathways of escape, mainly because you must take your eyes off your attacker. Better said, you must engage your peripheral vision to either monitor the attacker's movements or identify your path of egress. If those options aren't available, the need to determine any vulnerabilities of the attacker to open up a possible escape route.

Decide - This is your flight or fight cue. Based off the information you've obtained, the choice now becomes whether you choose to stay and fight or bug out. You do not want to freeze up and fail to make a lifesaving decision.

All of this can take place in a matter of seconds. It's a luxury if more time is granted for all of these steps, but oftentimes, that isn't the case. Hopefully, the mechanics and methods of putting your choice into action have been practiced and rehearsed to the point of appearing automatic.

The second acronym deals more with proper cover to make observations. Cover is not always available or too far outside a safe line of travel to be an inconspicuous option. However, if cover is available, it's best to use it, especially when observing people. People tend to become suspicious, paranoid, or even hostile if they discover they're under observation. Cover also becomes important during an active shooter event or when moving towards an exit exposes you to gunfire as you move.

SILVER

The best and safest way to observe is from behind cover. Good cover will have the following qualities:

S   - The cover will be *solid*.
I   - The cover will be *immoveable*.
L   - The cover will be *large* enough to hide behind.
V   - The cover will not impede your *vision*.
E   - The cover will provide *entry* and *egress*.
R   - The cover will *resist* or *restrict* your opponent's attack.

THE DAY THE MUSIC DIED...

Your ears provide a necessary link to many of the events happening around you. While there are many sounds we may find annoying or unpleasant, drowning those sounds out with music pumped into the ear canal severely limits your awareness. It is far too common these days to see several people wearing headphones or ear buds as they commute. I often ride the train to work and 90 percent of the passengers are actively using a mobile device, with 50 to 60 percent of those wearing ear buds or headphones. It astonishes me how so many people pay no attention to or acknowledge other passengers. Some don't even look up from their device when someone sits right next to them. Maybe I'm a bit too untrusting of my fellow man. However, I've read enough stories, watched plenty of news reports, and heard a good number of firsthand accounts to justify that distrust.

Your sense of hearing becomes much more vital at night, as your eyes must compensate for the decreased line of sight vision. Have you ever noticed how insects like crickets will stop chirping if you come close to their location? You can hear other animals scamper further away into darkness. Other times, you'll hear a dog bark to alert its master of someone too close to his or her property.

People do not purposely obstruct their vision, but that's not the case with their ears. Hearing is crucial for early detection of potential threats and risks. Photo courtesy of www.pixabay.com.

"The most dangerous person is the one who listens, thinks, and observes."

- Bruce Lee

CHIVALRY ISN'T DEAD, BUT...

One of my favorite modern interpretations of chivalry comes from bushcraft survival and SERE instructor, Matthew Tate. He once stated that if you open a door and allow your family to enter first, you potentially expose them to whatever events are unfolding inside at the time of entry. Sometimes you can't see or hear what is going on inside until that door opens. By entering first, he is able to quickly assess the general safety and determine if the activity within is safe and/or something he wants the rest of his family subjected to while there. It may not look chivalrous from an old school point of view, but it makes sense to do so. It's better that the perception of chivalry die rather than family members.

If things are acceptable with nothing out of the ordinary, he leads the way. If not, he uses a pre-determined "crash" word to alert his loved ones. The family doesn't need to ask any questions, they know through practice and drills that the crash word means it's time to leave. He uses his lead position to shield them from danger as they exit if things are already going sideways. If the potential for trouble exists, but hasn't occurred, they leave and find another place to go.

YOU SPIN ME ROUND...

Your senses and your ability to process the received information are your greatest risk assessment tools you have. Don't deliberately blind or deafen yourself with technological distractions, which sabotage and desensitize you to your surroundings. Don't limit yourself to the clichéd "head on a swivel" mantra. Every time I hear this phrase, I think of the 80s song, *"You Spin Me Round"* by Dead or Alive. The head on a swivel is a misnomer and tacticool catch phrase. It's also physiologically impossible, as the human skeletal system does not allow the head to rotate 360 degrees for a true swivel effect. A better observation method would be one that embodies the lyrics, "I can see clearly now...I can see all obstacles in my way" by Johnny Nash.

Therefore, incorporate a more encompassing PAN-TILT-ZOOM method of observation. PAN from left to right and right to left. You should be able to see an object or person directly behind you within your peripheral vision and provide 360-degree coverage. TILT your head up or down at stairwells, ramps, or escalators. Tilting can also minimize detection from facial recognition cameras if you're inclined to want to avoid being noticed or identified. ZOOM in on anything that is out of the ordinary until it can be explained or determined to be safe.

PAN - Sweep left to right/right to left slowly and methodically. Moving too fast makes your behaviors look erratic and suspicious to others. Pause where necessary, but attempt to complete full observational arcs.

TILT - Raise and lower your head while still utilizing the PAN motion. Watch as you approach underpasses, bridges, or other elevated structures. Use caution when approaching stairwells, tunnels, and confined spaces or narrow alleys.

ZOOM - Mentally and visually intensify your focus on objects or individuals that appear out of place, are lingering too long, or don't have a legitimate reason for being where they are or doing what they're doing.

Sometimes you cannot get a broad overview of an area before you enter it. This is most common with law enforcement and military personnel when performing raids or executing warrants in close quarters. Often times, officers and soldiers have to "pie" the room, observing and clearing small chunks based upon their line-up prior to breaching a room or building.

Another observation method is right-left-down-up. As our normal tendency is to read left to right, top to bottom, it forces the brain to pay closer attention to items or people within a particular space. It's quite effective, and being a writer, I can vouch for this method working extremely well as a proofreading tool. Used in conjunction with dividing an area into pie slices or manageable sections, this method lessens the likelihood of missing something important.

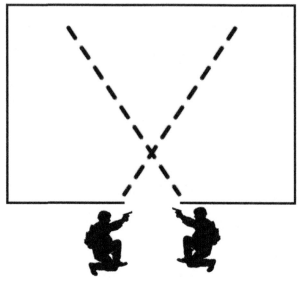

Each officer takes a designated slice of the room to clear and secure.
Illustration by author.

WATCH YOUR BACK

What happens when you heed all of the aforementioned advice? Is it possible for an attacker to circumvent your efforts to detect him and still set up an ambush? The answer is yes. Most successful ambushes are attacks that come from behind or the sides from a place of cover and concealment. Reducing an attacker's success means cutting off or disabling his advantages.

If you stop to get your bearings, tie a shoelace, read directions, etc., you should place yourself with your back against a solid, immoveable object. Preferably, a structure that is taller than you. Walls are the perfect choice. With your back up against a wall, you can be relatively certain that an attack from behind you is no longer a threat.

Males are more susceptible to attacks in public restrooms than women are. While women's toilets are surrounded by stalls for privacy, the urinals in male bathrooms offer little or no privacy. You're facing a wall, you're pre-occupied and relaxed, you're hands are obviously not in a defensive position, you can be "sized up" by all those entering the restroom, and you're incredibly vulnerable.

It is much safer, especially if you carry a firearm (open or concealed), to do your business within an available stall and commode. Although you're still technically facing a wall while urinating, you've now added three additional barriers. You now have privacy and can adjust a weapon holster. You no longer have to worry about someone noticing the weapon "printing" through your clothes. No one can size you up unless they've followed you into the restroom and have already made the decision to target you.

Public urinals are literally a no-go if you carry concealed. Photo courtesy of www.pixabay.com

Should you choose or need to sit, be mindful of the gaps between the floor and the partitions. Don't let your concealed carry weapon be made visible or accessible while you're sitting.

Everything echoes off the tiled walls of a public restroom. Use it to your advantage. Listen to everything. Listen to how the door opens and closes, footsteps across the floor, water running in the sink, toilet flushes, hand dryers, etc.

Readers may question why I focus on this and here's an ancient example. In 1 Samuel Chapter 24 in the Bible, it recalls the events of King Saul pursuing David. While in the Desert of En Gedi, Saul entered a cave to relieve himself. Neither King Saul nor the 3,000 men he had with him knew that David and his men were hiding in that particular cave. Because the cave was used to shelter sheep and goats, Saul's men carelessly chose not to perform a security sweep of the cave prior to Saul's entry. While Saul relieved himself, David crept up unnoticed and cut off a piece of Saul's robe.

Let that sink in for a minute and analyze the situation. Saul severely lacked situational awareness. He was complacent. His men were lazy and negligent. David was incredibly tactful and stealthy, waiting for the opportunity when Saul would be the most vulnerable and least protected. Had it not been for David showing mercy towards Saul (even at the protest of his own men who advised him to kill Saul), this encounter could have been deadly for Saul. David could have quite easily justified ending Saul's life in self-defense; as Saul had made attempts on David's life previously and failed.

Unlike David, your potential attackers will not show mercy towards you. David was offered the chance to prematurely gain the throne and kingdom of Israel. Your potential attackers will kill you for the contents of your wallet in an effort to secure their next meal or their next drug binge. With that in mind you must use all of your senses with ruthless and cunning efficiency.

Your Senses are your first primary tools of choice. Use them often, use them well, and use them unapologetically; for there is no law governing their overuse to the point of the legal definition of excessive.

WHEN THEY HIT YOU WITH THEIR BEST SHOT...

One of the more disturbing types of assaults during the past several years has been sudden, unprovoked assaults. These attacks were named the "knock-out game" by the media. According to media and news sources, it was being reported that teens were attempting to knockout unsuspecting victims with a single sucker punch to the head.[1]

While there were some reports of these types of assaults occurring, most of the reports were later found to be false or an urban myth. Law enforcement officials in major cities didn't deny the existence of these types of attacks outright or that the probability was low. Regardless of the probability, the video evidence that accompanied the news story were proof enough of the need to be ever vigilant.[2]

Your senses are your most powerful threat detection tools. The best thing is you always have them on your person. This means you can never forget to take them with you. Which is a good thing, because there are plenty of saboteurs out there wanting you to forget how to use them.

Citations:

[1]https://en.wikipedia.org/wiki/Knockout_game

[2]https://www.usatoday.com/story/news/nation/2013/11/26/knockout-game-myth/3729635/

SCRUTINY

Just like everyone else in the world, I have opinions on many different topics and subject matter. It should be no surprise to have an occasional dissenter to some of my held beliefs and opinions. My opinions, beliefs, and mindsets are a direct result of my own research, experience, and yes, cognitive bias. Because I choose the option to self-publish my work, I care very little if someone doesn't agree with my opinions or thinks they don't belong in a work of non-fiction. There is always someone who doesn't understand, appreciate, or tolerate differences in opinion. We are not capable as human beings of being absolutely homogeneous with no personal desires or incentives to provide meaning and purpose. As Maslow shows in his hierarchy of needs theory (refer back to Chapter 2, pg. 24), a utopia where everyone lives in peace and harmony is not possible without the complete disregard and abandonment of self-interest.

The one area of contention I often get feedback from is the topic of stereotyping and bias. To that end, I get the whole span from those who agree with me and those who disagree. Until someone convinces or forces people to all think and act alike through utilitarian social engineering at the expense of self-interest and personal goals, the likelihood of people rebelling against forced conformity and groupthink will continue.

People are a lot like breakfast cereals: there are a lot of varieties and choices out there. Some are bland, some are sweet, some are flakes, some are nutty, and yes, some leave a bad taste in your mouth. I can scrutinize and give preference towards any cereal I choose based on a specific grain, sugar content, texture, composition, organic ingredients, character on the box, gluten-free, manufacturer, price, whatever. None of these makes other cereals bad, less appealing, or nutritionally inferior in the eyes of others, but it may not be what I like. In addition to this, I also have the prerogative to change back and forth between cereals for whatever reason I have at any time. That's the true beauty of diversity. I can choose. Demanding I like every cereal is not diversity, it's totalitarianism. Inclusiveness is not diversity, either. Inclusiveness demands I buy every cereal, pour equal amounts from each box into my bowl, and happily eat the mixture set before me, regardless of the conflicting tastes, consistencies, or level of hunger. It's a waste at best and force-feeding at worst.

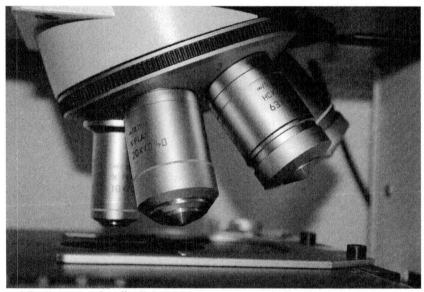

While we cannot legally discriminate against people based upon appearances and characteristics, you most certainly can scrutinize and observe behavior on an individual basis. Photo courtesy of www.pixabay.com

Here's another example: I would hazard a guess that no one with even the slightest of measureable intelligence would surrender his or her decision-making and personal preferences when choosing a spouse. Most people would never delegate the choice to someone else, let alone a government. Just imagine if the government chose your spouse, regardless of your preferences or even your desire to marry. Think of how potentially unhappy you would be in an arranged marriage of this kind? This is but one example of how large the role of bias exists in our lives. Therefore, when people say that *all* bias, scrutiny, stereotypes, and discrimination are bad and abolished, they themselves are guilty of generalizing the ability and freedom to choose.

It's easy to miss this yellow crab spider at first glance due to its colorations. Our brains, however, are hard-wired to detect differences. The spider's prey will not be so fortunate. Photo courtesy of www.pixabay.com

Most scrutiny and personal bias stems from a lack of trust. Trust is always earned and can be easily lost through deceptive practices and dishonesty. All it takes is one experience or interaction with a person to put up barriers and boundaries.

Ninety-nine percent of the time, this restricted access to friendship or future general civility is the result of displayed behavior of a negative nature.

There is level of irony in society that exists with the knowledge that most humans dislike uncertainty. Uncertainty is doubt. Yet, people demand that we unequivocally give the "benefit of the doubt" to people we don't know, haven't met, or haven't vetted. It's a catch-22 that will never go away. Then we also make the outrageous demand that other people not dislike us for whatever reason. For example, all across college campuses in the United States, the people demanding tolerance and acceptance for all cannot seem to extend that same level of tolerance and acceptance they demand. It reeks of hypocrisy and the average American can smell it quite easily. Our survival depends upon our ability to scrutinize and discern the people and things around us.

Scrutiny and a more than casual approach to observation are needed to detect the two deer hiding in this fallen tree. Photo courtesy of www.pixabay.com

You'd better believe I'd scrutinize the living daylights out of somebody until I've vetted them to my satisfaction. I expect people to do the same to me. There is no so-called privilege granting me carte blanche trustworthiness. The culture of political correctness neither agrees with this truth nor acknowledges it. You could also bet a year's worth of paychecks on a sure-winner that there are people who don't like my beliefs, my heritage, my ideologies, or me. I myself would take that bet any day of the week and twice on Sunday.

Stereotyping and bias are often summed up with the phrase, "That person ruined it for the rest of us." It's an inconvenient truth to accept that one's behavior can adversely affect others who have no direct link or association to you or your chosen behavior, but it sometimes does. It may not be right and flies in the face of those who wish to create a utopian world.

I can assure you, if I were to drive into the north side of Chicago at a particular time of day, I guarantee I would be scrutinized. If I want an authentic Chicago-style hot dog and I heard the best place to go was some hole-in-the-wall hot dog stand near the old Cabrini Green area, my presence there would attract attention and scrutiny. It wouldn't matter how well I could articulate my love for Chicago-style hot dogs or my desire to patronize the best place to get one. Some people wouldn't care. The only thing some would notice is that I don't blend in with the majority of the population there. My presence there could trigger a whole slew of verbal and non-verbal responses from the residents. It's simply a fact. Strangers are always met with some level of distrust. It's a defense mechanism and it's a prudent one; even if it means I'm on the receiving end of that scrutiny.

Your background, life experiences, and culture will determine the who, what, where, when, and how you scrutinize things that may become or have the potential to be a threat to you. The wider berth you choose to give someone walking down the street may be justified; or it may not. If someone's behavior doesn't line up with what society reasonably expects of what you reasonably expect; watch and observe him or her closely. Behavior is the catalyst for present and future action. *Sense, See,* and *Scrutinize* to cancel or confirm the threat and either carry on or prepare to *Suppress* threatening behavior.

SIGNS

Comedian Bill Engvall is famous for his "Here's Your Sign" routine. His sarcastic observation of people and their apparent inability to apply logic and critical thinking skills have made his audiences roar with laughter for a couple of decades. Most of his teased "victims" are merely making poor attempts to break the conversational ice or determine how something happened by stating the obvious.

Just like many of those who find themselves to be the butt of Engvall's jokes, we often look for more signs and clues to answer the obvious. We can blame this behavior on many things such as the need for additional information, trying to avoid stereotyping or making false assumptions. However, I posit that it may be our mind's attempt to entertain the denial phase of the Kubler-Ross model of a "This can't be happening to me" event.

Another example is the lyrics from the song "Signs" by The Five Man Electric Band. The chorus goes, "Signs, signs, everywhere signs...blocking up the scenery, breaking my mind...Do this, don't do that; can't you read the signs." The song is true in the fact that there are signs everywhere. Our choice to observe and obey/disobey the warning then determines our safety.

Job sites and construction zones have several warning signs to notify people about the dangers existing within a certain area. Unfortunately, high crime areas never have nice metal signs and placards to help make wise choices. Photo courtesy of www.pixabay.com.

The intention of some signs to promote or dissuade a certain behavior sometimes border on irony to the point of idiocy. One example that immediately comes to mind is one sign I saw years ago when stationed in Okinawa, Japan. Just before the entrance to the US Marine Corps base Camp Butler, there was a sign written in English with the Japanese translation below it reading, "The Posting of Signs is Strictly Prohibited." The irony was hilarious to me, as well as the underlining idiocy. They violated the edict of the sign in an effort to enforce it.

Hindsight has an overwhelming track record of perfect vision. When studied long enough during the course of an investigation, it identifies human shortcomings and procedural error. Despite its intention to detect and piece together events along a particular timeline to prevent future reoccurrence, it often becomes an abusive, counter-productive tool. It is used to administer punishment for failing to have some vague, immeasurable level of clairvoyance into the circumstances leading up to the incident. An event resulting in an unacceptable outcome is subject to far greater scrutiny. People make mistakes. They always have and always will. All we can reasonably expect from others and ourselves is a best effort, an admission when we fail, and acceptance for the consequences of our actions.

Sometimes signs cannot prevent a violation or a circumstance in which it was intended to stop. The sign size, color, phrasing, symbols/symbolism, picture, shape, and language are still subject to some level of individual interpretation. It is irrelevant if the interpretation is not understood, the utilitarian approach of "everyone gets it" doesn't prevent tragedies from happening.

A typical gun-free zone sign.

Gun-free zone signs are viewed in many different ways. One person sees and obeys the sign without hesitation because of their complete agreement. One person sees it as a ban preventing the carry/use of a Beretta M92F semi-automatic handgun or whatever handgun silhouette is displayed, but all other guns are permitted. Criminals see this sign as a welcome mat to release carnage on helpless and unprepared soft targets incapable of fighting back or stopping the attack.

"Common sense is not a gift; it's a curse, because you have to deal with everyone who doesn't have it."

- Unknown

BODY LANGUAGE

A rudimentary study of body language often gives clues to a person's motives, intentions, and disposition. Body language further gives context and meaning to the things people say and how they say it.

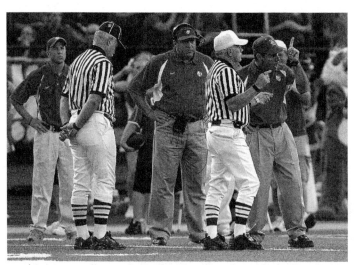

What can this image tell you about the situation through the interpretation of body language? Who's upset? Who doesn't like confrontation? Photo courtesy of www.pixabay.com.

68

The following key indicators can serve as an early warning system to a potential threat. It is important to remember these body language cues do not always mean an attack is eminent; nor is a single cue indicative of intentional, violent behavior. Persons with mental disabilities can often display several cues at once and not be a threat. Adolescents trying to appear street-wise and tough may adopt certain body language as a means of posturing. However, when confronted by a person with real or imagined authority, the adolescent backs down. The key word here with all body language and signaling is *immediate* and *eminent*.

Common Pre-Force Indicators:

• Taking a fighting stance
• Flailing of the arms
• Hesitation in answering
• Repeating of the question
• Absence of vocalization
• Fake yawn
• Flanking
• Pacing
• Stretching
• Scanning (for either escape or witnesses)
• Rapid blinking
• 1000 yard stare
• Lying eyes
• Long drag on a cigarette
• Physical signs of stress
• Refusing to submit to arrest
• Tightening of jaw or clenching of teeth
• Weight shifting
• Backing up

- Mouth breathing
- Chanting/singing to self-motivate or intimidate
- Fist clenching
- Shoulders roll forward
- Chin drops; knees bend
- Protective instincts[1]

STEREOTYPES AS SIGNS

We live within a society and historical age that demands all stereotyping, discrimination, and prejudice be unilaterally shunned and removed from everyday practice. This zero tolerance policy and attitude is both unrealistic and dangerous. Most of our decisions, both good and bad, are based on experience or the experience of others. If I were to walk down the street and mugged by someone of a specific gender, with a specific accent, a specific skin tone, a specific hair color, and a specific body type and appearance, would I use these specifics to describe the individual to the police? Absolutely. Those specific attributes could narrow the list of suspects, resulting in a greater chance of apprehending the person responsible. The police find and arrest the suspect based on those specifics.

To think that all stereotyping and profiling is evil is simply asinine. There is no other way to describe an intentional choice not to use information to better identify someone. If you are to meet a new business client, do you not give a description of yourself so you and your new client will know they're meeting the right person? If you are separated from a travelling group, don't you give descriptions of the people you were with to authorities to help reunite you?

It's ironic that some people demonize the use of certain demographic information to apprehend suspects and known criminals, but don't think twice about providing such information to apply for grants or some form of governmental aid or assistance program.

SUSPICIOUS BEHAVIOR

When I was completing my Certificates II and III in Security Operations in Australia, the class was reminded often that suspicious behavior is, "Absence of the normal, presence of the abnormal." This mantra is a great example of establishing Anomaly and Baseline. Although most people can detect suspicious behavior, few can articulate it into words well or under pressure.

The ABC's of suspicious behavior are:

Anomaly
Baseline
Context

Despite the listed acronym, the baseline must be established first. Your baseline will vary in depending on the environment. Baseline is an initial set of observations and data regarding a person or place.

Secondly, deviations from the observed baseline must be confirmed as being relevant and complimentary baseline information or an anomaly. Anomalies are any additions, subtractions, or noticeable changes to the baseline. This means that not all anomalies are bad or dangerous just because they vary from the baseline. This leads us to the next step in the behavior cycle.

Lastly, interpretation of received data provides context. Not every anomaly requires an escalated response beyond the additional observation. That observation may detect something through body language or behavior or may determine there to be no threat, with no further action required on our part.

It's important to understand that scrutiny should be restricted solely towards a persons' behavior, not physical characteristics. Behavior is the key component in lawfully executed scrutiny.

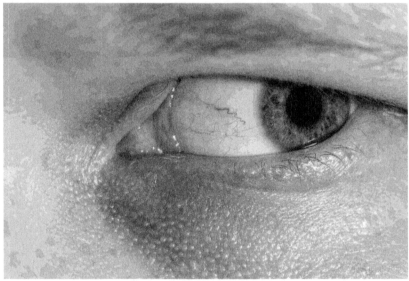

Shifting eyes are but one behavior that most people associate with suspicious behavior. Photo courtesy of www.pixabay.com.

The argument we often get from people of interest (POIs) is they accuse security of targeting them. However, in most cases, the person's body language invites an inquiry from security. A person initiating a stare at security personnel often instigates this. In our culture, staring at someone is considered impolite. We sometimes oblige them by staring back. The result then becomes them becoming defensive, raising their voice to draw attention to themselves, and portraying themselves as the victim. This is a form of provocation designed to escalate a trivial occurrence into a conflict.

They often work themselves up into a frenzy, becoming aggressive and abusive, thereby forcing security personnel to intervene in the interest of public safety and enforcing the conditions of entry. The retailer has already notified us that the person of interest has committed theft and given security a description of the alleged suspect. However, a person's body language cues security. Their behavior becomes more suspicious. The suspect begins walking faster and erratic, while looking over their shoulder attempting to avoid confrontation and apprehension.

More S Word alliteration warning signs...

All of the following words can have obvious red flags associated with them and can be indicative of potential warning signs to areas or persons you should actively avoid. Again, context after determining the baseline will dictate whether the detection of one or more of the following is reason to increase our level of situational sense and pay closer attention to our surroundings.

Strobes - Flashing lights are a good indication of not wanting to be where police, fire, and emergency response/paramedics are actively attending an incident.

Sirens - Just like the flashing strobes on response vehicles, the siren is heard often before the lights are seen. Sirens may mean help is on the way, but as I stated back in the first chapter, they may arrive too late.

Strangers - Anytime you find yourself around a person or people you don't know, you should have already begun a course of action, or at the very least, have elevated your awareness. Not all strangers are *immediately* dangerous and some strangers never evolve into a legitimate threat.

Sanctions - Travel bans and tourist "no-go" zones are places to avoid actively and adamantly.

Squalor - Squalor is filth. Any place that is unkempt and dirty, with an apparent lack of concern regarding its appearance is a clear indication that you don't want to be or shouldn't be there.

Sharps/Syringes - Anytime you find dirty needles or drug paraphernalia in areas where they shouldn't be, you need to quickly monitor and assess where you're at and the best path to get to a more hygienic area.

Stragglers - People loitering about with no indication of legitimate reason to be where they are can be a good indication that things need to be observed more cautiously.

Sentries - Gangs typically use younger gang members as watchers for potential threats from the police and rival gangs, as well as potential buyers and runners.

Security - Security personnel are legitimate, licensed, and employed guards who are present as a deterrent in an attempt to prevent criminal activity from occurring.

Squads - Squads are typically groups of 8-14 people. Obviously this many people converging on your location, regardless of how many are present with you is cause for concern.

Surveillance - CCTV cameras, alarm monitoring systems, and active security are typically found in areas subject to frequent crime.

Smoke - The old adage, "Where there's smoke, there's fire" cannot be taken for granted. If the signs for trouble are present, chances are it's there waiting to fully ignite.

74

Swearing - Despite being less taboo, swearing is usually indicative of someone being upset and is a method of conveying that anger prior to an escalation of violence.

Squabbles - Squabbles are arguments that can potentially become much more aggressive and violent. Watch for increased swearing, name-calling, verbal abuse, posturing, and confrontational body language as cues for violence to erupt.

Shooting - If you hear gunfire, you should be heading in the opposite direction. If you find yourself the intended target of gunfire, you need to put distance between you and the shooter, moving in jagged movements that are also rapid and unpredictable towards a place of cover. Moving targets are more difficult to hit. If you are armed, prepare to resist the attacker's advances from behind that cover.

Snares - Snares are temptations and enticements. Most of the troubles we find ourselves in are the result of us giving in to temptation by staying too long, trying to catch a glimpse of the action.

Symbols - Symbols and symbolism, especially those associated with gangs and the occult are found usually in areas where a particular gang/occult group operates and/or has claimed as their territory. Being caught in one of these areas can be quite dangerous.

By clearly identifying early warning signs will aid in solid decision-making and risk avoidance. Use every sense and visual cue you can to recognize danger before it becomes unavoidable.

Citations:

[1]Delarosa, Aurelio, Comani Facebook post, January 11th, 2017, https://www.facebook.com/teamcomani/?fref=ts

SABOTEURS

It is no coincidence that my previous books address the importance of the human senses. This book will be no different in that aspect. Our senses, the sensory organs used to collect data, and our cognitive learning used to interpret the received data, are central to our survival. It is important to realize the inherent power we give to things that effectively dull our senses. I refer to these things as awareness saboteurs.

Billboards, video screens, and digital marquees are among many of the saboteurs that create sensory overload and lower our situational awareness.
Photo courtesy of www.pixabay.com.

77

The infamous cellular phone has sucked our attention away from so many other important things in life like no other device in the 21st century. Paired with a set of ear buds and being handheld, it has drastically reduced the effectiveness of three of the five senses. Photo courtesy of www.pixabay.com.

Saboteurs, in regards to situational sense, are things that suck our attention away from our surroundings or inhibit our ability to respond alertly to situations occurring within our immediate environment. These saboteurs draw our senses away with distracting stimuli. Sometimes this is done as a deliberate misdirection by an attacker or perpetrator. Sometimes it is through an unwitting accomplice. Sometimes, it is a person within our own family demanding our time and attention based on their inability to obtain what they want or require without assistance.

In my previous book, *Gray Man*, I briefly explained how the Reticular Activating System (RAS) filters and manages the massive amount of sensory input to the brain. Depending on our environment, certain sights and sounds trigger a response or are filtered out, being labeled irrelevant or non-threatening. For example, police sirens usually evoke an attentive or inquisitive response from someone living in a rural area. However, in an urban environment, people's responses to the siren may be more ambivalent unless they have summoned the police or the police response has immediate or pertinent correlation to their present situation.

FORMS OF AWARENESS SABOTEURS

The easiest way to remember Awareness Saboteurs is the alphabet. The letters A, B, C, D, E, F, and S start each word relating to internal and external attempts to reduce your awareness. Some of these saboteurs may be beyond your ability to control, while others can be managed with a proactive and decidedly vigilant mindset.

Ambivalence

Ambivalence, means to show no care or willful disregard for something that, to a reasonable person, should be worthy of having a high value or esteem and a desire to attain or retain possession of a particular thing. Simply put, it is an "I don't care" attitude. This type of reckless attitude puts you and others around you who are subject to your care or protection potentially in harm's way. This type of saboteur relies heavily on the partnership it has with distraction. Ambivalence is sometimes deemed an interruption to a perceived higher priority task. Often, the task is not a higher priority. A perfect example is a teenager responding with "I'm Busy", when summoned to take care of their chores. We often find them watching TV or playing a video game.

Body Limitation

Our physical bodies can only perform tasks when we are healthy, well nourished, well rested, and properly hydrated. Any systemic compromise to our physiological being reduces our ability to recognize and respond appropriately to changes occurring within our environment, regardless of whether those changes are perceived as good or bad. We need proper diet and regular exercise. Some body limitations due to disease may beyond control, but doesn't serve as an excuse to be lax.

Complacency

We are creatures of habit and enjoy life much more when things require less work or effort on our part. As things become increasingly more convenient through technological advances, we tend to rely more on technology and governmental services to provide more and more of the comforts that enable us to do less work.

Preoccupation with technology puts us at risk when our attention is drawn away from potentially dangers. Photo courtesy of www.pixabay.com

Distractions

Distractions come in many different forms. Today, the greatest distraction is the modern Smartphone or other type of handheld electronic device. These seemingly small things create some of the biggest distractions because our eyes are focused on a viewing screen rather than the happenings within our immediate vicinity. Other distractions can include children, daydreaming, flashing lights, music, people we find either sexually attractive or repulsive, etc.

Environment

Our everyday environment can produce so many stimuli that we can sometimes feel overwhelmed. Other times, it can put us in a state of hyper-awareness where we potentially over-react or inappropriately respond to stimuli we are presented with as we go about our business. Most often, the over-saturation in stimuli reduces our ability to sense what is important in regards to being aware of our surroundings. For example, walking into a strong head wind blows the sound of approaching footsteps from behind away from you. Someone yelling a warning from behind you may not be heard as well under the same conditions. Rain, snow, and fog are other examples of environmental impairments.

Familiarity

The more familiar we become with a person, an action, or a process, the more comfortable we become with its presence. Familiarity doesn't necessarily develop into complacency, but rather a lack of vigilance and attention to detail.

"Familiarity breeds contempt only when it breeds inattention."
- George Santayana

Substances

Of all the potential saboteurs, probably the most dangerous are substances. There is a specific reason why they are added is their ability to influence the only other saboteur types that we can control. To add to their potential danger even further is the fact that cartels, sex traffickers, serial rapists, and organ harvesters often slip substances into food and drinks in order to incapacitate and capture their victims. The results are often heartbreaking, bloody, and tragic.

Substances can be further split into three subcategories. Because of their detrimental effects on the body, these are added to the ongoing S word alliteration conceptual model to highlight their importance.

All sorts of foreign material and substances can be introduced into food and food ingredients. Bruce Willis' character in the movie Red 2 said, "If you don't make it, you don't eat it." While a bit extreme, the advice does have some merit. Photo courtesy of www.pixabay.com.

Sustenance - This includes all food and beverages designed to maintain core energy levels and homeostasis. The types of food we eat can cause energy spikes or be so nutritionally deficient that it shouldn't really be considered food. I'm just as guilty as the next person is, as I have a fondness for several foods that doctors, nutritionists, and diet advocates discuss with distain. In some cases, food is sometimes tainted with poisons or drugs as a more deceptive way to introduce a foreign substance into the body. Much more common, however, is the introduction of bacteria and germs that make our situational sense vulnerable as our immune system attempts to fight off sickness and infections.

Stimulants - Legal stimulants like caffeinated drinks and energy drinks are in abundance. Like many Americans, I also partake and sometime over-indulge in my consumption of coffee, iced tea, and soft drinks. Sugar is also another compound that acts as a stimulant in some people. Of course, the most dangerous are the illegal/illicit drugs such as cocaine, crack cocaine, and methamphetamines.

Never accept beverages or food from strangers. Always keep a watchful eye on your beverage or have companions monitor it if you leave the table for any reason. Photo courtesy of www.pixabay.com

Sedatives - Sedatives are what I refer in classes as the typical depressant drugs such as alcohol and barbiturates. These drugs are designed to relax or slow certain physiological functions. They often reduce motor skills and mental alertness, among other side effects. As mentioned before, alcoholic beverages are often spiked with so-called "club drugs" like Rohypnol, liquid ecstasy (GHB - gamma hydroxybutyric acid), and ketamine.[1]

There are so many illicit, illegal, and controlled substances out there and I willingly admit that I'm no authority on the subject of drugs. The Internet provides more information than I can offer. Familiarizing yourself with street-names and drug effects is a good starting point if you want more information. I've added some websites in the resources section in the back of the book.

Drug addiction is often depicted as unhygienic and risky behavior. The danger, besides the obvious health concerns, is the feelings of euphoria sought out by users make them either oblivious or needlessly hypersensitive to their surroundings. Photo courtesy of www.pixabay.com.

It is highly advisable if you hold a concealed carry weapons permit, that you should never be willfully ingesting alcohol or any other depressive substance while actively armed. Save your responsible consumption of alcohol for at home where the likelihood of conflict is substantially reduced. It should also go without saying that illicit drugs should never be physically in your system. Nor should they be in your presence. The only exception would be in an official law enforcement capacity, as part of a sting operation or as recovered evidence.

"Make yourself sheep and the wolves will eat you."
- Benjamin Franklin

Here is a short list or potential saboteurs to situational awareness:

Cellular phone or other handheld electronic device
Alcohol
Billboards
Window displays
Drugs
Music
Video screens or television
Public address announcements
Physical contact
Animals or pets
Children
Loud noises (tires screeching, sirens, car horns, fireworks, etc.)
Food and food smells
Eating
Hygiene/Grooming/Toilet
Suggestive clothing (or lack of clothing)
Behavior outside accepted social norms and culture

Technology has the tendency to make us lazy. We have cars with multiple sensors and self-driving or correcting features. We don't feel the need to check our mirrors, check our blind spots, or pay more attention to our behavior behind the wheel. It not only reduces our practical driving skills, but also our diligence in maintaining the vehicles we drive. We don't even bother to check fluid levels or tire pressure unless a warning indicator illuminates on the display panel; alerting us to do so. This problem, unfortunately, is not isolated to our treatment and operating of motor vehicles.

Our over-reliance on technology hasn't done us any favors. People don't read maps or plan routes; we choose the path of least resistance, the fastest route, or the cheapest route. I'm not saying that we should intentionally and utterly abolish all of these mentalities, but it is no coincidence that things worth having in life require effort, take time to develop, and cost us something. You should view your personal safety in a similar manner. It will require some of your effort, time, and money. The amount of each you dedicate to your protection and the protection of your loved ones will determine the quality and effectiveness when those skills are called upon in a dangerous situation.

Technology's purpose should be to create synergy and to develop, maintain, and strengthen a collaborative partnership between people. In some instances, it has created compartmentalized disunion and separation. In a way, situational sense is synergy between common sense and situational awareness, hence why the book is titled *Situational Sense*. Both are needed individually, but when combined, they are greater than the sum of their individual contributions.

Obviously, you'll never be able to eliminate all of the potential saboteurs to your ability to use and maintain situational awareness. However, being able to identify potential distractions will lessen the likelihood of being caught by surprise, startled by abrupt changes to your baseline, or ambushed.

Citations:

[1]https://www.medicinenet.com/date_rape_drugs/article.htm

SECTION THREE

PREPARE

STUDY-SLEUTHING

Prolonged, in-depth studying and gathering intelligence is sometimes a luxury that field operatives, security personnel, and those in close personal protection don't have. While they'll have briefings prior to the start of an operation, risk assessments, and SMEAC, these informational meetings don't replace the need for individual study and training. SMEAC, for those not familiar with the term, is an acronym for a five-paragraph battle order, with each paragraph highlighting a particular stage. These five stages are Situation, Mission, Execution, Administration, and Command.[1]

Orientations and inductions only provide brief overviews, as well. Obviously, we need to be able to adapt and overcome challenges presented to us. Coming into a situation knowing we don't possess all the information needed to perform our assignments safely and efficiently is not the most ideal scenario. We should correct this to the best of our ability. Therefore, studying through common methods such as reading, research, and attending training courses/classes are essential to preparedness.

"Underestimation of a person's intelligence, strength, and aggression just makes you less prepared. Expect anything from anyone."

- Sonya Teclai

Study should always be a dual-purpose activity. First, it should increase knowledge and skill-sets to strengthen you. Second, it should expose weakness in your enemy. Enemy is a strong word, but in life and death situations, the will to survive should overrule any societal obligation to civility in regards to your attacker. An attacker isn't going to heed gun-free zones, legislation, feel-good policies, ethics, social norms, Common Law, or the Ten Commandments. Therefore, you must resolve within yourself to prepare mentally, emotionally, and physically for any situation you may encounter within your daily life, regardless of the environment and the conditions presented.

Studying requires more than just reading, but reading is always a good starting point. Seek out practical, competent training from certified instructors. Practice the skills learned with like-minded people. Photo by author.

"By failing to prepare, you are preparing to fail."

- Benjamin Franklin

There is no limit to the subject matter or quantities of such that can be studied and applied. Reading is often the first step in acquiring foundational instruction and introduction to a particular subject. The subjects can vary from practical, hands-on skills all the way to abstract philosophical subjects that can influence or shift your mindset or worldview regarding how you approach life situations.

Part of studying is the development of a personal contingency plan. Some people call it an emergency action plan, response plan, or a SHTF (S**t Hits the Fan) plan. The name really isn't important. What is important is that you have one. It can start out as simple as asking, "What will I do if this happens?" The plan can be as elaborate and specific as needed, as long it is actionable. You may not be able to think about every potential threat, but having a basic foundational plan will help.

"I love it when a plan comes together."
- Colonel Hannibal Smith, from the television show, The A-Team

It is a wise decision to plan ahead and have a workable plan. Photo courtesy of www.pixabay.com

Not all threats will be in the form of physical violence. Take, for instance, fires and building evacuations. Both carry significant risk to you, even death, but still are not viewed in the same light as violent confrontation.

Many corporations and companies have an emergency color code to notify employees of potential threats to safety. While there seems to be some shared, definitive color choices for certain types of threats and emergencies, there remains several that differ from company to company, even within the same industry.

Hospitals and medical clinics attempt to coordinate their color codes, but they differ drastically from other industry guidelines. For example, a CODE WHITE would often be warning staff of someone committing an act of violence, where in the security industry, this type of emergency might be called a CODE BLACK.

Fire or smoke	**CODE RED**
Evacuation	**CODE ORANGE**
Bomb threat	**CODE PURPLE**
Personal threat	**CODE BLACK**
Internal emergency	**CODE YELLOW**
External emergency	**CODE BROWN**
Medical emergency	**CODE BLUE**
Lost Person	**CODE GRAY**

An example of emergency color codes. Illustration by author.

If you've purchased this book, chances are you're already aware of the dangers present in this world. Knowing what to study and accessing information about the places you frequent or plan to visit is important. This is where the concept of sleuthing becomes involved. Floor plans, evacuation routes, exit locations, and fire suppression equipment are sometimes posted on websites of the current property owner/management company. Due to the increased threat of terrorism, many places like sports stadiums, airports, museums, and monuments, these websites may not offer access to these layouts.

	Negligible	Marginal	Critical	Catastrophic
Certain	High	High	Extreme	Extreme
Likely	Moderate	High	High	Extreme
Possible	Low	Moderate	High	Extreme
Unlikely	Low	Low	Moderate	Extreme
Rare	Low	Low	Moderate	High

A typical Risk Matrix.[2]

A risk matrix is a threat assessment tool to aid in determining and preparing for the likelihood of crisis events or emergencies. Because its use would be subject to several variables, which may or may not entertain a certain level of paranoia or worry, a risk matrix may not be the most reliable tool to accurately assess the dangers one may face. Potential threats would be construed as highly subjective, with a particular threat being much more likely to one individual than another's or that of a group of individuals.

Another common example of risk matrixes are those used by governments to inform its citizens regarding the threat of terrorism. While they many seem vague or non-specific in terms of the what-when-where concerning targets, they do provide an easy to understand approach to communicating information to large groups of people. Because of the universal understanding of color symbolism throughout the world, having a small matrix infused with color codes ensures a maximum amount of people will be able to comprehend the message.

Terror Threat Tables

Color	United States	US Military FPCON[3]
RED	Severe	DELTA
ORANGE	High	CHARLIE
YELLOW	Elevated	BRAVO
BLUE	Guarded	ALPHA
GREEN	Low	NORMAL

Color	United Kingdom	Canada	Australia
RED	Critical	Critical	Certain
ORANGE	Severe	High	Expected
YELLOW	Substantial	Medium	Probable
BLUE	Moderate	Low	Possible
GREEN	Low	Very Low	Not Expected

One of the more difficult aspects of gathering information is that many of the methods required to obtain that information can be construed as suspicious. Taking notes and photographs in addition to viewing posted information such as emergency exits, fire and evacuation routes, muster areas, and fire suppression equipment are keys to determining how safe you feel in certain environments.

Sleuthing not only entails the above information, but also includes investigating statistical crime reports and current trends. This isn't done to promote fear-mongering, but it is necessary to see what types of crimes are prevalent in your area. The unfortunate downside is that some of the usual sources are becoming less and less trustworthy. The nightly news, regardless of which bias preference you hold, can no longer be trusted to unequivocally tell the truth and do it objectively. Furthermore, statistics gathered by local police departments and reported to the FBI are still susceptible to skewed numbers or suppressed data to support agendas.

I have viewed several security posters in various shopping centers, universities, convention centers, and airports throughout my career in various security related occupations. They all label and target anyone taking notes, taking photographs, collecting information, perceived loitering, aimless or erratic travel, and challenging/testing security measures.

While the Johari Window is an often used as a self-awareness technique, I see little reason why it cannot be adopted into a situational awareness technique.

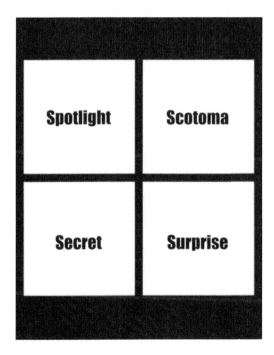

Modified Johari Window for Situational Awareness.[4] Illustration by author.

Spotlight - This is a threat that you and most people in the same vicinity know about and can easily see.

Secret - This is a threat that only you are aware of and others are oblivious.

Scotoma - This is your blind spot threat. Others can see this threat, but you cannot.

Surprise - This is a threat that neither you nor others know about.

"One cannot simultaneously prepare for the worst case scenario and the best case scenario."

- Brian Stewart Germain

The purpose of studying is to gain knowledge and insight into things that we know we are lacking. The more knowledge we have and increasing our ability to recognize training gaps allows us to focus on those areas in order to avoid the scotoma (blind spot) and surprise attacks.

Citations:

[1] https://en.wikipedia.org/wiki/Five_paragraph_order

[2] https://en.wikipedia.org/wiki/Risk_matrix

[3] https://en.wikipedia.org/wiki/Force_protection_condition

[4] https://en.wikipedia.org/wiki/Johari_window

STRATEGY

While strategy and study may appear on the surface to address the same thing, the two are significantly different. An effective strategy cannot be conceived and carried out without study. Proof in point is thieves. Thieves study the characteristics of potential victims. They make their target selection, based on factors such as time of day, victim age, ability of the victim to resist or pursue, weather, bystanders/witnesses, etc. All of these factors determine their chance of success and the amount of potential risk incurred during the commission of the crime.

While not all criminals study and plan due to various levels of experience, intellect, or other factors such as drug use or impairment, most criminals have criterion they use to select prey. In the same manner, it is wise to have a strategy in place as a starting point in a violent encounter. Events may not escalate or deescalate with the desired outcomes, but you'll be better equipped than someone with no plan at all.

"I read, I study, I examine, I listen, I think, and out of all that I try to form an idea into which I put as much common sense as I can."

- Marquis de Lafayette

Effective strategic planning involves learning everything you can about an enemy, their tactics, and their modus operandi, in order to be several steps ahead of your enemy in thought and action. Photo courtesy of www.pixabay.com

DECISION MAKING

Our desires to pursue what we want when we want it often produce many poor decisions in life. There's an internet meme floating throughout cyberspace containing a black and white photograph of Dean Martin holding a drink with the caption: "Good judgment comes from experience. And experience? Well, that comes from poor judgment." You may easily recall several disappointments linked directly to the following of an impulse in the moment.

Most of us learn from our experiences, either because of our success or because of our failures. When faced with a life or death situation, it is not a time to accept the possibility of mistakes that come from a lack of preparedness or sufficient training.

There are four different decision making processes mentioned within this text. All four were previously mentioned in *Gray Man*, but are added, as they are quite relevant for the sake of context. They are GOFER, PDSA, DECIDE, and OODA. These decision-making methods are extremely important when used in conjunction with the interpreted and filtered stimuli we receive from our environment or circumstance.

GOFER - In the 1980s, psychologist Leon Mann developed the GOFER model, based on the earlier research of another psychologist, Irving Janis.

<u>Goals:</u> Survey values and objectives
<u>Options:</u> Consider a wide range of alternative actions
<u>Facts:</u> Search for information
<u>Effects:</u> Weigh the positive and negative consequences of the options
<u>Review:</u> Plan how to implement the options[1]

PDSA - During the late 1940s and 1950s, Dr. W. Edwards Deming developed the PDSA cycle and still considered the quality control strategy used by businesses worldwide. The straightforward simplicity of <u>Plan, Do, Study, Act</u> helps explain its appeal.

<u>Plan</u> - Plan the test, including a plan for collecting data.
<u>Do</u> - Try out the test on a small scale.
<u>Study</u> - Analyze the data and study the results.
<u>Act</u> - Refine the change, based on results from the test.[2]

DECIDE - In 2008, Kristina Guo published another decision-making methodology.

<u>Define</u> the problem
<u>Establish</u> or <u>Enumerate</u> all the criteria (constraints)
<u>Consider</u> and <u>Collect</u> all the alternatives

100

<u>Identify</u> the best alternative
<u>Develop</u> and implement a plan of action
<u>Evaluate</u> and monitor the solution and examine feedback when necessary[1]

The OODA Loop - The OODA loop (<u>Observe</u>, <u>Orient</u>, <u>Decide</u>, and <u>Act</u>) has been an important development in how we understand cognitive human response and behavior during a crisis situation.

This decision-making methodology is still popular. Since its development came from Colonel John Boyd (1927-1997), it's often popular within military and veterans circles, as well as many critical elements within law enforcement agencies.

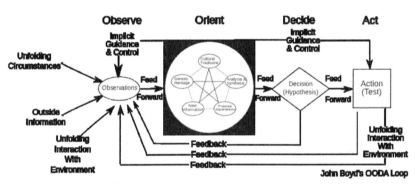

Colonel Boyd's decision cycle, commonly referred as the OODA Loop.
https://en.wikipedia.org/wiki/OODA_loop

It is my opinion, and possibly the opinion of others, that it is much more prudent in some circumstances to *Orient* first, followed by *Observe*. If you don't orient yourself to the surrounding culture while including your past experiences, how do you know *what* to observe? The possibility to receive or interpret information incorrectly can slow the appropriate decision and delay or stop the correct action.

"The key is to obscure your intentions and make them unpredictable to your opponent while you simultaneously clarify his intentions."

- Harry Hillaker,
Discussing Boyd's OODA Loop in *Tribute to John R. Boyd*[3]

RUN HIDE FIGHT

Run, Hide, Fight is the strategy promoted during an active shooter event on many government websites, including www.ready.gov.

RUN

Exit Strategies

The decision for flight or fight should take into consideration as many factors as possible. As stated earlier, fleeing is often the best option in many situations. Fleeing does not translate automatically into running or sprinting. It could mean taking an alternate route, a detour, or less congested route.

Here are a few definitions to help you understand the reasons how and why people should avoid certain environments and situations when considering an exit route.

Bottleneck - Just as a glass bottle is tapered at the top and grows out to the wider base, bottleneck is a tactic forcing people from a confined entry/exit point into a wider area. The reverse is also true and limits peoples' routes of escape to one narrow, highly congested, slow moving mass. The result is a greater number of injuries and casualties.

Choke Point - A choke point is essentially the reverse of a bottleneck. Forcing a mark into a choke point allows surveillance to positively identify the mark, restrict or reduce the speed of their escape/evasion, or limit the direction of available travel.

Funneling - Funneling is a tactic for forcing prey into a singular direction with little or no means of detour or backtracking, usually from a wider area to a much narrower area.

Field of View - Any military veteran and combat strategist will tell you it is best if you can occupy the high ground. Being in a higher position allows you to see potential threats from farther away and allows you to see more of the landscape to determine routes of travel, identify threats, and locate paths of egress and cover/concealment.

There is a third option beyond fight or flight, but it will leave you injured or dead. Some people, when faced with a surprise violent encounter, simply freeze. They can neither run nor fight. Avoid this behavior at all cost. The best solution is to a have an identifiable and rehearsed contingency plan.

HIDE

In the event that escape is not prudent or possible, hiding is the next best option, according to www.ready.gov. The idea of waiting for an attacker to find you doesn't sound very appealing. I think the situation would be worse if I were forced to hide with others. You cannot anticipate or control their actions. They may scream as soon as the attacker rattles the door. You may have one in the group who calls to his wife to offer a mushy, guilt-ridden goodbye instead of keeping his phone off.

If you have to hide, hide by yourself. Most active shooters are looking for maximum carnage. They want to find large groups of people to kill. Hunting for stragglers takes too much time, especially if they're mindful of their target body count to make the nightly news and immortalized in history for the briefest of moments. In addition, if you fail in keeping quiet you've only placed your life at risk, not a bunch of other people who may not have the same level of determination to fight back.

"I'd rather be tried by twelve than carried by six."

- Randy Alcorn

FIGHT

When no other option is left, you must fight. You must fight with everything you have. If your attacker still ends up victorious, make him suffer for it. If he manages to walk away, make sure he is bloodied, exhausted, or his killing efficiency is severely decreased. Preferably, you would want him unable to walk away, but alive, for legal reasons.

However, if your attacker leaves no other choice, take his life. He has already proven himself in your eyes of his desire to do the same unto you. Killing is an ugly business and fortunately, I've never had that fight come my way. Several of my colleagues and mentors have had to make that awful decision. The reason they are still here today is that they planned, prepared, and performed the necessary decisions and skill-sets to stay on top of the topsoil. I hope I never have to use the skills I've acquired. All I can reasonably do is actively avoid places and people I believe will manifest into an undesired problem. What cannot be avoided must be prepared for through solid decision-making and training choices.

PRIORITIZE WHAT'S IMPORTANT...

The Eisenhower Decision Matrix is one method to determine if events need your immediate attention, tasks that can be delegated, and those that can ignored for a period of time. In a crisis, it will be urgent to escape, but maybe not important to run to facilitate that escape. You might have to drop your newly purchased grocery items. While it may have cost a reasonable amount of money and would be inconvenient to have to repurchase, during an active shooter incident, you probably wouldn't be too concerned about leaving the items.

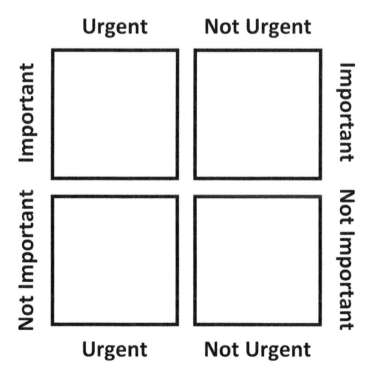

The Eisenhower Decision Matrix.[4] Illustration by author.

Having a workable plan and solid decision-making processes in place will assist you in prioritizing what needs to be done during a conflict or crisis to make sure you survive. I hope that your decisions will help you avoid the conflicts before they have the chance to manifest.

Citations:

[1]https://en.wikipedia.org/wiki/Decision-making

[2] http://www.ihi.org/resources/Pages/HowtoImprove/
ScienceofImprovementTestingChanges.aspx

[3]Hillaker, Harry, *Tribute to John R. Boyd*, January 28, 2015

[4]https://en.wikipedia.org/wiki/Time_management

10

SKILL-SETS

The most important thing about skill-sets is not to get caught up comparing and critiquing skills, but rather spending the necessary time, effort, and discipline to acquire and revisit those life-saving skills. You must be able to deploy those skills decisively and properly when the circumstances warrant them. The only way this can be done is through regular practice.

Many taught skill-sets are multi-faceted or incorporate additional beneficial training during sessions. For example, cardiovascular exercise is often included in some martial art training. The Israeli martial art Krav Maga comes to mind. When I first enrolled in Krav Maga, various fitness exercises were introduced in between sparring exercises and striking drills to keep the heart rate up. It was also done to help students "push through" fatigue and adds the element of physical stress in which the student must learn to manage effectively. Not all martial art styles do this and not all gyms/dojos incorporate it, but it makes sense to provide the additional cardiovascular fitness training.

Martial art training is a very personal decision and unfortunately, the selection of any particular discipline is subject to heavy bias and personal preference on behalf of both practitioners and detractors alike. If you put forty masters of forty different martial arts disciplines, you will get forty answers as to why one is the best and why the other 39 are not. Systematically asking each person will produce that same result 39 times. Therefore, you must make your discipline decision equipped with as much knowledge as you can; knowing fully that whomever you seek counsel and advice from is going to be biased to a certain degree.

As with any physical activity, certain skill-set training is going to be more rigorous than others are. Therefore, you should decide carefully; taking into consideration the level of physical exertion required to participate. Initial exhaustion can be just an issue of conditioning to build stamina, however, if major health issues manifest or that continue after a couple of weeks, you may need to reduce some of the activity. The best advice is to visit your doctor and have them assess your current health prior to engaging in an intense training regimen.

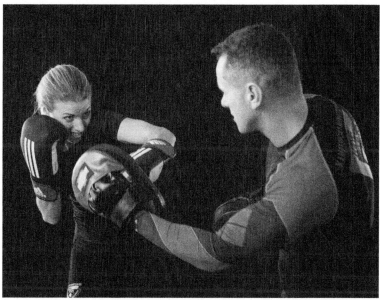

There are hundreds of fighting methods, martial art disciplines, and self-defense courses available. Choose a method that allows you to train effectively, learning the necessary skills. Photo courtesy of www.pixabay.com.

I can neither recommend nor discourage any specific martial arts training, as I believe there is always something useful to be found within the varying disciplines. However, I will say this, if your sole intention is to use the skills for strictly defensive purposes, you'll find that almost all martial art disciplines make use of both counter-attacks and offensive techniques. They are taught in conjunction with the defensive tactics. This means you'll be taught both offensive and defensive techniques that have the potential for lethality. So make no mistake, there is no exclusively defensive discipline. You must be prepared to offer up violence to stop the violence place upon you.

Another important consideration of choosing a particular discipline is, as you age, your body is going to be less effective and resilient. When you're young, you may be able to handle the physical stress of some of the grappling-based disciplines. You may eventually see a reduction of physical strength, which may hinder your ability to grasp and control an attacker. However, as you get older, getting up from the ground may become more difficult. Growing old is hell, but let's face it, not growing old means you didn't survive. The wise choice is to compliment your fighting skill-set with a secondary discipline.

Training and acquiring skills is essential to developing a combat mind-set. The easiest way to describe what is necessary to prepare for potentially deadly encounter is this: Skill-sets develop the physical requirements and mind-sets develop the mental and emotional requirements. Both are easier said than done. Developing skill-sets and mind-sets are deliberate acts requiring dedication to the particular craft and self-discipline to continue in a forward trajectory of progress.

A phrase that was often used (and still used) by some trainers is the term, "muscle memory". I dislike the term, as muscles do not have memory, they can only respond to nerve impulses. The repetitiveness of controlled, intentional, and disciplined movements are conditioned in the mind, executed by the body, and when done enough times, become a habit or trained response to a given stimuli.

"The body cannot go where the mind has not gone first."

-Brian Stuart Germain

Shooting, whether recreational or defensive, is a perishable skill, which must be practiced often to ensure, speed, safety, and shot placement can be properly and practically executed when needed. Photo courtesy of www.pixabay.com.

Cooper's States of Readiness/Combat Mindset

Lieutenant Colonel Jeff Cooper was one of my first indirect teachers regarding situational sense. As my father was a police officer, he routinely stressed the importance of being mindful of our surroundings to my brother and me. He attended Gunsite in the late 70s and owned many of Cooper's training videos. My favorite was the Combat Mindset video and its teachings are still in effect today as I pass those lessons onto my children. Cooper's

Color Code of readiness (as he referred to it in a Gunsite training video) was simple in theory and explanation. I immediately was able to implement it upon entering high school. I've included his *Color Code*, elaborating on them slightly.

Condition White: This refers to having a state of willful/unconscious distraction to events occurring in your immediate proximity. The effects of sleep deprivation, alcohol consumption, or drug use (regardless of type) all impair your ability to focus or identify threats; making you unready/unlikely to detect or defend against ambushes.

Condition Yellow: I mentioned the Pan-Tilt-Zoom observation method back in Chapter 4. This is the basis of Condition Yellow. You are coherent, relaxed, and calmly observing your proximity for potential threats. You are aware of who and what is around you on all sides. Threat development is low/improbable and unspecific, although you are mentally engaged and ready should a situation arise. Cooper once stated in the aforementioned video, "You can comfortably live in Condition Yellow for the rest of your life." This should be your primary condition when awake.

Condition Orange: Threat detection has occurred and you are actively assessing specific individuals who are now displaying threatening behavior or mannerisms. You are positioning yourself, watching the hands of the hostiles, identifying potential weapons, and formulating a fight or flight response based upon the scenario. You are prepared both mentally and physically for an altercation.

Condition Red: Adrenaline dump has occurred and you are actively engaged in fight/combat situation. You are decisively and actively opposing an adversary through a prescribed or practical use of force continuum in order to stop the threat or escape and evade.[1]

"If the day ever comes where you have to fight for your life, the only thing that will determine the outcome is if you ever trained and prepared for that fight."

- Tim Kennedy

The skills you learn and put into practice today will be the ones that will preserve your life tomorrow. Acquire as many skills as you can. Train often and without apology, because it is certain an attacker will never apologize. Only your training and tenacity when a situation warrants it will make your adversary sorry he chose you as his intended victim.

Citations:

[1]https://americanpatriotrealitycheck.wordpress.com/survival-pages/combat-mindset-the-cooper-color-code/

11

SYSTEMS

Weapons and weapons systems are a necessary force multiplier when confronted with multiple attackers, or attackers who are larger than you are or have a distinct, articulable advantage over you. One thing criminals thrive upon is the notion that law-abiding citizens do just that; abide by the law.

With that said, you must ultimately decide what weapons you are willing to accept the consequences for carrying or NOT carrying. I am not a lawyer and cannot provide legal advice. Nevertheless, as I mentioned at the beginning of the book, you are responsible for your own safety. You are responsible for your choices and conduct. You are responsible for the methods and procedures you use administer that safety. You are responsible for your training and your competency.

Lastly, you are responsible for the consequences of the outcomes that arise from the use of force. Everyone likes the flashy, seductive look of the response to violence, but then turn their heads away from the truth of the responsibility. If there has ever been a foundation that has eroded faster than that of common sense, it is the foundation of responsible actions paired with accountability.

PROJECTILE WEAPONS

Projectile weapons are weapons that allow the distance or space between combatants to be greater than with traditional fighting weapons. This is a broad category of weapons, which include spears, the bow and arrow, crossbows, slingshots, or any type of object that can be hurled or thrown towards an adversary. If you've ever wondered why there has always been an ever-present push for gun control and restrictions on projectile weapons, it can be traced as far back as to crossbows during the Middle Ages.

Due to the social class structure, the idea of a weapon powerful enough to pierce the armor of knights, lords, and noblemen land in the hands of serfs and commoners holding no nobility was outright condemned. A crossbow could wipe out an entire ruling class and subsequent heirs, prompting Pope Urban II to ban the weapon in 1096.[1]

That is the very reason why firearms are under so much scrutiny from elites and those holding political office or some form of ruling control over large groups of people. The firearm is the fiercest foe to tyranny and the forms of government seeking to rule with absolute authority and disregard to the natural rights of man.

Firearms

Firearms are the great equalizer within American society. All around the world, however, the affinity towards the firearm and its subsequent industry is much maligned and despised. While there is great political debate on who should be allowed to possess firearms or who shall be granted the authority to determine that possession, one this is certain, the firearm demands respect. In a society where citizens are allowed to arm

116

themselves, criminal are force to reevaluate the risk-benefit ratio of their anti-social and deviant behavior.

In order to best accomplish the goal of self-protection, the key factors of portability and concealment must be considered. Therefore, when discussing firearms within the realm of situational sense, the type of firearm predominantly used with respect to the above-mentioned factors is the handgun or pistol.

Firearms are classified as a weapons system. Beyond the obvious marksman and safe handling skills needed, proficiency in malfunction clearing, minor repairs and regular maintenance should be included. Photo courtesy of www.pixabay.com.

While shot placement, caliber, and penetration all play a part in the overall effectiveness of the firearm, it is important to realize that the use of a firearm is to stop the further continuance of violence. If lethal force is justified and the perpetrator dies as a result of wounds sustained during the commission of a crime or the subsequent apprehension; the intent always and forever should be to end a lethal confrontation; never to seek revenge, retaliate, or offer swift justice.

Contrary to both current and long-standing media narratives, armed citizens and the police are not wishing death or executing preemptive judgment on the individual who commits a crime. That doesn't mean those feelings or desires are non-existent, but generally speaking, feelings of revenge and the resulting submission to those feelings are never allowed to manifest. However, this doesn't stop Hollywood from using those emotions as the underlying motive in the plots of numerous action/adventure movies.

Law enforcement professionals and citizens don't operate within or tolerate vigilante style justice. It is simply that a situation has escalated to the point where no other form of persuasion or non-lethal force has convinced the offender to immediately stop his or her unlawful behavior. When it is clear that law enforcement personnel or citizens cross the line into the realm of brutality with the motives of revenge or retaliation, they become subject to the same criminal prosecution as everyone else.

The risk to personal safety of a person or persons must be considered as being *immediate* with serious injury, grave peril, or death occurring if the action towards the victim(s) is not stopped immediately.

PROPELLANT WEAPONS

Propellant weapons are those weapons that disperse and introduce chemical irritants into the respiratory system, the mucous membranes of sensory organs, or both. Typical examples are oleoresin capsaicin (OC) spray, commonly known as pepper spray, CS gas, also known as tear gas, and CN gas (or MACE). Depending on the state, all three are available to civilians for self-defense use.[2] Propellant weapons are classified as non-lethal and can work effectively with proper training.

MELEE WEAPONS

Melee weapons refer to any number of traditional and non-traditional weapons used in direct combat.[3] Often these weapons offer different methods to obtain the same result: incapacitation of an enemy. While not seen as scary by modern society due to their primitive origins, make no mistakes, these types of weapons are just as deadly as a firearm.

Axes, swords, spears, and knives all belong to the large family of edged weapons. Photo courtesy of www.pixabay.com

Edged/Pointed Weapons

Edged and pointed weapons are ones that I personally am most fearful of coming into contact with, whether on or off duty. I have had colleagues stabbed with scissors. We've found drug needles in handbags, knives in pockets; you name it. People with edged weapon training are much more formidable than someone just pointing a firearm. The knowledge they possess regarding target areas and strike zones means that they have the potential to cause permanent, catastrophic, or lethal damage. While the firearm may incapacitate or kill at a greater distance, a blade is up close and personal.

Trauma Weapons

These are your striking weapons used to create blunt force trauma to a particular part of the body. Successful strikes produce hematomas (bruises/internal bleeding), bone fractures, and joint dislocations. The head is often the primary target, as effective melee weapon use produces the secondary objective of unconsciousness, making the recipient vulnerable to further attack or inability to fight back.

Firearms and edged weapons are not the only weapon threats out in society. There are people who use a wide array of improvised items that based on first glance and their intended purpose may be perceived as non-threatening. Photo courtesy of www.pixabay.com.

"The first murder weapon was a rock."

- Unknown

VOLTAGE WEAPONS

Stun guns and tasers fall into the category of voltage weapons as their primary function is to distribute a high voltage/low amperage electrical current to the body. The received electrical charge is painful, and may produce temporary paralysis or loss of motor movement in the limbs. Recipients often shake uncontrollably, resembling a seizure. Their effectiveness is often called into question, causing many states to legislate ownership restrictions or issue bans on the use, possession, and sale of voltage weapons. Tasers shoot out prongs into an attacker. Both barbs must penetrate clothing and contact the skin in order to deliver the shock effectively.

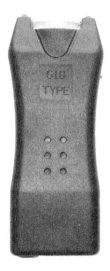

Older versions of voltage weapons still exist, but many of today's shock devices are smaller, more compact, and concealable. Photo courtesy of www.pixabay.com

IMPROVISED WEAPONS

If the thought of an armed attack with items most people consider weapons isn't frightening enough, you must consider further the possibility of confronting someone with an improvised weapon. An improvised weapon is any item in which the original intent and/or design of the item is not to be used as a weapon. However, opportunity and availability are usually the two governing principles dictating whether an item can be used as a makeshift weapon or not.

Despite the majority of knives in this picture, there are also other potential improvised weapons. Photo courtesy of www.pixabay.com.

The following is just a short list of everyday items that have been used to both commit crime *and* deter criminal attacks.

Scissors
Screwdrivers
Needle-nosed pliers

Pens
Automatic center punches
Pencils
Plastic cards
Rolled coins
Marbles
Glass bottles
Small figurines/statues
Ball bearings
Canes or walking sticks
Umbrellas
Pry bars/demolition bars
Newspapers or magazines
Hot beverages
Caustic liquids
Aerosols
Belts
Chains
Baseball bats
Golf clubs
Tennis rackets
Hockey sticks
Metal pipes
Hammers/mallets
Keys
Flashlights
Picture wire
Neck lanyards
Shoe laces[4]

Making assumptions about whether or not something is a weapon or could be used as a weapon is a two-edged sword. Based on the sheer number of items that have the potential to become a weapon in the trained or prepared hands of another person, we must always assume that everyone we see has some type of weapon on them. Their knowledge of how to use an item effectively as a weapon may be questionable or even non-existent, but the fact remains that they have it in their possession.

It is also important to note that the lethality of certain items can and will vary. Factors such as strike placement, number of strikes necessary to incapacitate, puncture depth, etc. may allow for escape without death.

The next section focuses on empty hand combatives systems. When discussing suppression methods in Chapter 13, it is important to remember, however, that not all martial art disciplines are strictly utilizing empty hand techniques. Many martial arts also focus on a particular weapon, such as swords, knives, or melee/impact weapons. Nun-chucks and bow staffs frequently come to mind. Their deployment has a distinct, measureable outcome advantage in terms of suppression methods.

Before we jump into the Suppression methods of Chapter 13, Chapter 12 reinforces the idea that we should think before we act, therefore, we'll look at Street-Smarts next and attempt to lay some foundational common sense. The insistence of engaging our brains to make quick decisions and use critical thinking skills must come first in the Execute phase.

Citations:

[1] https://militaryhistorynow.com/2012/05/23/the-crossbow-a-medieval-wmd/

[2] https://www.cityofpalmdesert.org/departments/police-department/helpful-tips/self-defense-tear-gas-pepper-spray

[3] https://en.wikipedia.org/wiki/Melee_weapon

[4] http://www.returnofkings.com/97318/14-self-defense-tools-to-use-where-weapons-are-banned

SECTION FOUR

EXECUTE

12

STREET-SMARTS

The opening quotations in the book by two of my childhood heroes, John Wayne and Bruce Lee, are intended to provoke and remind the reader of the importance of making wise decisions. Decision-making is a process, with multiple facets, variables, and analyses. It is often difficult to apply exact procedures and protocols because every circumstance has its own set of unique opportunities and drawbacks to consider. However, there exist some basic, universal principles that allow us to make rapid, assertive, and effective decisions regarding our own personal safety.

"Common sense is not so common."

- Voltaire

Common sense is a personal trait routinely joked about being in short supply nowadays. I wish it weren't true, but far too often, we see the decline in our neighborhoods, our schools, and our society, rather than a steady indicator of its existence. In the same fashion, we see a distinct lack of critical thinking and logic skills. One merely needs to look at a jar of peanut butter and read the bold print allergen warning: CONTAINS PEANUTS. I should hope so, that's why people buy peanut butter. It makes sense that people with peanut allergies wouldn't buy it. However, the consumer packaging craziness doesn't end there.

127

There are warnings on the packaging of frozen pizzas stating, DO NOT EAT FROZEN. From this it is clear to see that the governing authorities have deliberately put a moratorium on Darwin's "Survival of the fittest" posit and pass countless regulations and legislation to protect stupidity as if it were an endangered species.

We can observe the many ways people consume the nightly news, as they gullibly accept force-fed bias and agenda-driven stories without question or further investigation. They sponge and absorb whatever information the talking heads feed them. Unfortunately, many engage in this type of "intelligence" gathering in an attempt to be informed. Nevertheless, in order to judge events rightly, one must make the effort to hear more than one viewpoint.

If spray-painted artwork is not part of a recognized or authorized art display, entering into areas with large amounts of graffiti is not advisable, especially at night. Graffiti often appears in places lacking CCTV monitoring and may mark gang territory. Photo courtesy of www.pixabay.com.

"What is common sense isn't common practice."

- Stephen Covey

I am just as guilty as anyone else is, capable of being sucked into an intellectual void of offsetting opinions and engaging in a futile battle defending a position against someone equally passionate and stubborn as I am. Social media platforms are an evidential cesspool of false narratives, photo manipulation, and unverified accounts regarding much of what we see in our personalized newsfeed. The danger lies where we fail to research and find substantiated facts, choosing instead to accept whatever propaganda and lies are put before us.

"We have too many intellectuals who are afraid to use the pistol of common sense."

- Samuel Fuller

Listening, learning, and following directions go hand and hand. My father always used to say that some people "Can't pour piss out of a boot; even if the directions were written on the heel. But, they can read the directions in three languages." Although he didn't coin the phrase, I remember him also saying, "Never try to make anything idiot-proof. Someone will come along and deliberately breed a better idiot."

A majority of the times where we fail to use what is referred to as common sense stems from two very broad categories. These categories are not knowing how to do something or the willful exclusion of or bypassing necessary steps. In other words, taking shortcuts.

Another dangerous pitfall is perception. Perception is another one of these mental double-edged swords. Your perception of a situation and how you mentally process and interpret things directly affects your response. Likewise, other people's perceptions of your actions can cause them to make wrong assumptions or misconstrue your intent. Intent is the keyword in many situations and can be very subjective when viewed through the lens of perception. A good way to minimize mistaken intent is to mirror your actions while verbally articulating your intent.

Synchronize your *Skill-Set*s and *Systems* deployment with *Speech.* This basically means show <u>and</u> tell. Your actions are showing a behavior that for the purposes of this book, are considered justified. However, not every spectator will see the entire scenario or situation unfold from start to finish. Oftentimes, the provocation is not seen, only the response or reaction. CCTV (Closed Circuit Television) camera footage can only show so much, and only if the cameras were positioned in the direction of the incident. Camera footage is often grainy in appearance, making it difficult to see with 100% clarity. Sometimes it gets even worse when zoomed in to focus on someone's hands or the introduction of a weapon. While people may not be able to see the events, some will hear what was being said and will provide statements accordingly. This is why you must speak clearly what you're commanding the attacker to do and articulate the consequences if he chooses to ignore those commands.

"We all run the risk of thinking that people have common sense sometimes."

- Hozier

The problem isn't so much that people aren't thinking. The problem is people aren't physically stopping an action long enough to perceive the potential problems and consequences. They see the reward of what they're trying to accomplish and basically "keep their eyes on the prize."

We often see safety sacrificed on the altar of convenience and efficiency. Yes, there are ways to accomplish tasks faster. We improvise the screwdriver handle for a hammer and the tip for a pry bar, merely for the sake of not climbing down a ladder, going back to the toolbox, or buying the proper tool for the task. Does it work?   Yes, but did it compromise our safety, our workmanship, and the reliability of the tool for later use? Maybe not initially, but repeated actions become habits, and habits have a reputation of turning into dangerous things later.

"People all over the nation are starved for honesty and common sense."

- Ben Carson

Telling people of their need for common sense is much easier than equipping and teaching them how to do it. However, there are two positions I want you to consider. First, if you feel that you don't have common sense in this particular realm of self-defense and situational awareness or want to develop it further, find a mentor. Despite being an author and reluctantly accepting the accolade of subject matter expert, doesn't mean that I don't make mistakes. Nor does it mean I have an endless fountain of common sense and wisdom, or that I know everything about a particular subject. I am just as fallible as any other person is.

The second is, if you do have common sense; be a mentor. By helping others, you sharpen your own skills and retain information as additional compensation for your efforts.

We often fall into the same common sense pitfalls because we believe that we are smarter than the last person who tried the same action. We pretend to understand and take into account all the variables, thinking we won't make the same mistake. It's like doing the same things repeatedly and expecting a different outcome. We foolishly believe the conditions are the same, the circumstances are the same, the components are the same, and the characters are the same.   When we make egregious assumptions like those, we put ourselves at a greater risk. We must never assume that we are immune to the consequences simply because nothing happened to the other person.   Nor should we assume victory because we followed steps 1 through 4, when the other person only made it to step 3.

The greatest life-changing and life-preserving form of wisdom and intelligence is knowing when we don't have the necessary wisdom and intelligence. The greatest benefit comes when we challenge ourselves to obtain and learn those things we didn't know.

13

SUPPRESSION

In order to stop an act of aggression or violence, it may require us to resort to the same or greater amount of violence to suspend or suppress the aggression exacted towards us. Self-defense laws vary from state to state, as well as country to country. Most legislation have just enough to be considered broad for the sake of meeting possible contingencies, but then also specific enough to define penalties for actions that cross into any "gray area". The same level of discretion it grants you is the same level of discretion the police and courts will use to determine your justification or the lack thereof in any situation.

"The best personal defense is an explosive counter-attack."
                                                          - Jeff Cooper

The judicial system is a two-edged sword at best. It can save your life or take it. It can acquit you or condemn you. It can reward you or punish you. You must determine in a split second what action (or inaction) you will take and then accept the consequences of that choice. Inaction can result in sustaining needless injuries, permanent damage, or even death. The alternative can also produce the same results. You can make a justifiable decision to counter the violence against you and still be on the losing end. The list of possible unknown variables within any given scenario wreak havoc on our decision making process and therefore, must have some basic parameters in place.

Within the concept of suppression, we find the Force Continuum. It is also referred to as Use of Force or Deadly Force. All counter-measures to end the violence perpetrated against you must be necessary and reasonable. In addition, they cannot cross over into the realm of excessive and revenge-driven.

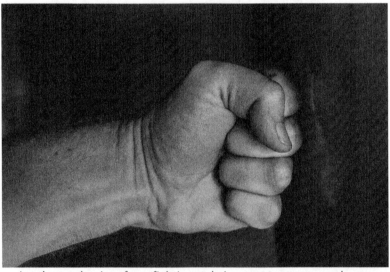

Learning the mechanics of any fighting style is necessary to properly suppress or end a physical conflict situation. It is a combination of knowing where to strike, when to strike, and how to strike. Photo courtesy of www.pixabay.com.

There are two basic criterions for suppression: *Necessary* and *Reasonable*. If you can effectively articulate your actions and show or prove justification, the better off you'll be if legal action is taken against you.

Necessary - Defined as an urgent, required response to a dangerous or life-threatening situation where injury, maiming, or death is an eminent or immediate result if no action or intervention is taken.

Reasonable - Defined as a logical and expected response to a situation where another person would act in a similar way under the same conditions when presented with the same set of circumstances.

Fear and adrenaline are emotional and physiological responses respectively. Fear of loss becomes a powerful incentive when paired with the body's automatic endocrine system response of "dumping" adrenaline into the bloodstream. However, the advantage it may make available during a threat doesn't fair as well in the courtroom. The emotion of fear is very subjective; as what one person fears may not be feared by others or to the same degree or intensity when a situation arises. Training and other factors may also determine the levels of fear felt and articulated by individuals.

Law enforcement personnel are well versed and trained regarding their respective department's use of force policy. However, this is not often discussed in civilian operated self-defense courses. Not knowing the legal definition of "reasonable and necessary" can put you at the defense table in a courtroom. Photo courtesy of www.pixabay.com.

There is insufficient evidence or proof that humans possess the ability to consciously interrupt both the nervous and endocrine systems to regulate the release of adrenaline into the bloodstream. However, both prosecutors and defense attorneys seem to convince juries that someone can just turn it off at will or correctly self-administer a suitable dose of adrenaline. While there are cases where "the heat of passion" becomes a mitigating factor, most people don't rely on this as a solid defense in court.

"Bite, kick, scratch, gouge out eyes; and if that doesn't work, fight dirty."

- Harry Dermody

Another point of contention is navigating the murky waters of our justice system. While justified under the law to suppress violence against you, there are those who would use the law to prevent you from suppressing that violence. Photo courtesy of www.pixabay.com.

As stated earlier, one of my early self-defense influences was the late American Pistol Institute/Gunsite founder and

Marine Corps veteran, Lieutenant Colonel Jeff Cooper. His book, *Principles of Personal Defense*, was one of the first books I read as I navigated my own struggle through adolescence being bullied throughout junior high and high school.

In this writing, the concept of suppression has more to do with the acknowledgement of its necessity rather than the mechanics or the execution of it. Every situation is different, with differing variables contributing to or complicating the overall execution. The only way to minimize the variables and avoid those becoming unnecessary hurdles to overcome is to practice your skills often.

Furthermore, you must commit physically and mentally to the act of suppressing the threat all the way through to completion. You cannot change your mind or waffle between two decisions without putting yourself in greater danger than when you first were presented with the threat. Pulling back strikes can provoke further attack, as now the initial attacker can claim, albeit wrongly, that he is now threatened and under attack. Furthermore, hesitating and holding back punches may lead onlookers to believe that you're not in as much danger as you believe you are.

DISCLAIMER: Strikes targeting areas on the skull are considered dangerous and/or lethal from most self-defense instructors and use of force continuum trainers. Strikes to these areas often produce instant, incapacitating pain, loss of sensory perception, unconsciousness, or death.

STRIKE SECTORS (body)

As stated earlier in this book, fighting is the last resort. It is considered the last resort because your options to reduce physical harm or injury have been systematically eliminated by you or your adversary. When the time for action and violence come, you must strike hard and repeatedly until the threat stops or the attacker no longer continues in the commission of the crime against you. Strike sectors are areas on the body that, when struck violently and decisively, should slow or stop an assault against you.

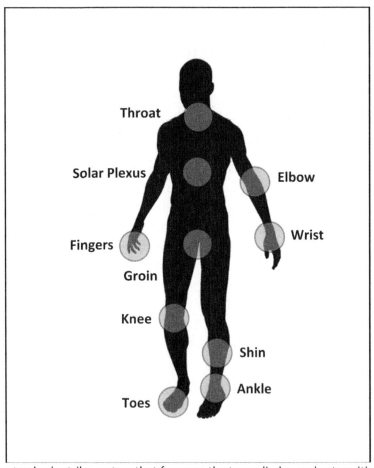

The ten body strike sectors that focus on the torso, limbs, and extremities.
Illustration by author. Silhouette figure courtesy of www.pixabay.com

"...Whatever comes, face it on your feet."

- Robert Jordan

Throat - Striking the throat can cause involuntary coughing, gagging, gasping, and difficulty breathing. Grasping and squeezing an attacker's throat can potentially crush the larynx, causing asphyxiation and death.

Solar Plexus - Striking the solar plexus rapidly inverts the diaphragm, causing pain and difficulty breathing.

Elbows - Striking the elbows can cause intense, numbing pain that often feels like a burning sensation extending from the radial nerve down into the fingertips.

Wrists - Striking or grasping the wrists allows a defender to halt certain hand strikes and provides a contact point to gain custodial control over an assailant.

Fingers - Striking or grasping/twisting the fingers can produce dislocations, hyperextensions, and fractures. Damage to the fingers may prevent the formation of a closed fist for striking or the pinching/grasping ability of individual fingers.

Groin - Striking the groin produces intense pain, causing the body to involuntarily bend forward or drop to the knees; further exposing the body to secondary strikes.

Knees - Striking the knees and the surrounding areas can cause major dislocations, fractures, hyperextensions, and ligament/tendon damage that may or may not be permanent. Knee injuries tend to incapacitate attackers immediately and prevent them from standing, chasing you, or fleeing to escape.

Shins - Striking or raking the shins with the side of a shoe or boot can cause instant pain, bruising, and skin abrasions. Well-placed kicks or strikes can produce fractures that incapacitate quickly.

Ankles - Striking the ankles can produce sprains, hyperextensions, and fractures; resulting in noticeable limping all the way up to complete structural failure where the person cannot apply any body weight on the affected foot.

Toes - Stomping on the foot and toes can break the small bones in the foot; making it difficult or impossible for an assailant to walk, run away, or pursue you.

STRIKE SECTORS (Skull)
Any counter-attack aimed at these points may result in you having to explain or defend yourself in court, justifying your actions to be considered an act of self-defense.

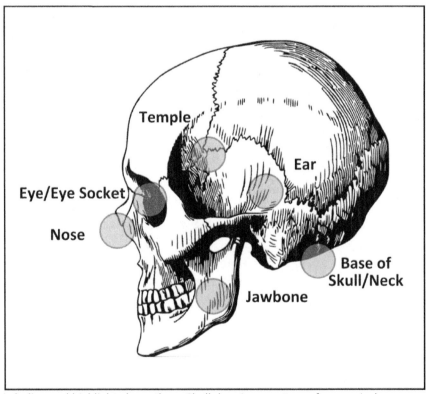

Labeling and highlights by author. Skull drawing courtesy of www.pixabay.com.

Temple - Striking the temple area can fracture the fissures of the skull, causing trauma to the brain, dizziness, and loss of consciousness.

Eyes/Eye Sockets - Striking or introducing a foreign object into the eye causes immediate blindness that is painful and ranges from temporary to permanent vision loss.

Nose - Striking the nose can produce an immediate flow of blood as well as involuntary closing and tearing from the eyes. Powerful palm heel strikes driven upwards can fracture the nasal portion of the skull and penetrate the brain cavity; resulting in severe head trauma and death.

Ears - Striking or slapping the ears can rupture the eardrum causing immediate pain, ringing in the ears, loss of hearing, loss of equilibrium (balance), and loss of consciousness.

Jawbone - Striking the jawbone can dislocate the mandible (jaw) from the rest of the cranium. Other damage such as self-inflicted bites to the tongue, broken/dislodged teeth, and in some cases, unconsciousness can occur.

Base of Skull/Neck - Strikes to the base of the skull and neck are potentially deadly, as these strikes can sever the spinal column, cause severe trauma to the medulla oblongata, resulting in brain damage, paralysis (both full/partial and temporary/permanent), unconsciousness, or death.

METHODS OF SUPPRESSION

As the Strike Sectors have been discussed, it seems fitting to mention the methods of suppression or the manner in which strikes are administered to an attacker. This section will coincide with the various types of available weapons mentioned earlier in Chapter 11 to administer strikes.

Striking - The use of hands or other body parts and/or melee weapons to stop an attacker.

Slicing - The use of blades (knives or swords) to sever muscle, tendons, or veins/arteries to stop an attacker.

Stabbing - The use of daggers or other pointed objects to puncture critical organs and create internal hemorrhaging to stop an attacker.

Shooting - The use of firearms to penetrate the structural integrity of the body to cause massive tissue trauma, hemorrhaging, and organ failure to stop an attacker.

Suffocating - The use of chokes to restrict the intake of oxygen into the body to stop an attacker.

Submission/Subduing - The use of grappling or openhanded restraints to hyper-extend joints and restrict natural body mechanics and movement, causing intense pain to stop an attacker.

"There was no such thing as a fair fight. All vulnerabilities must be exploited."

- Cary Caffrey

The above quotation is the mantra you must adopt. If you want to survive, you must use whatever suppression method, weapon(s), or tactics necessary to defeat your attacker.

SPECTATORS

The Spectators factor in the execution phase is a bit of a wildcard. As criminals often wait for their intended victims to be alone in the more brutal crimes such as murder and rape, having someone present to witness the crime is highly unlikely. Even if there were a witness present, there's no guarantee that person(s) would or could offer any assistance. It is a sad reality today, that when people find themselves in trouble and need of assistance, any bystanders present are more inclined to pull out their smartphones and video the event for a future social media post, rather than offering practical help or rescue.

While it would be far better to have active spectators, who, compelled by moral decency, were present to intervene and rescue, people may not be available or inclined to come to your assistance. Therefore, you must always prepare and act as if no one is coming to help you.

LIGHTS, CAMERAS, ACTION - The Hollywood Principle

The easiest way for me to describe the Spectator concept is to think of Hollywood. During film production, movie directors often call out the commands for "Lights, Camera, Action" for a particular scene. At each command, each phase would be turned on or set into motion. These three elements must exist in some capacity for spectators to engage in assistance, rescue, witnessing, or objective/subjective analysis after the fact.

LIGHTS - In order to provide the lighting necessary to capture the events, we should rely on as much natural and artificial light as can be produced in the vicinity. This also means we need to actively avoid locations where inadequate lighting is present. We find a great number of attacks happen at night or during low light conditions. Criminals exploit the lack of light because identifying people is much more difficult when there is insufficient lighting. It is easier to hide in the increased number of shadows, making ambushes more common and successful after nightfall.

Traveling at night is often a necessary risk. However, choosing routes and locations that are well-lit helps mitigate some of the risk. Photo courtesy of www.pixabay.com.

CAMERA - Surveillance cameras can often seem like a double-edged sword in modern society. The idea of being visually tracked from point to point via CCTV (closed circuit television) doesn't sit well with most people. CCTV, when it functions properly, serves as a passive witness, electronically documenting and time stamping our movements and providing a chronology of events. While cameras may seem like an effective deterrent to most law-abiding citizens, they are not without limitations.

Cameras that are offset mounted are most likely have a rotatable field of view. Photo courtesy of www.pixabay.com

Cameras such as the two pictured above are typically static/positional; meaning the cameras are pointed at a particular location. Photo courtesy of www.pixabay.com

145

<u>Old tech vs. New tech</u> - Many businesses or facilities may have a CCTV system in place for surveillance. However, older systems may be using cameras with lower resolution and reduced or no zoom capabilities. This makes "seeing" what takes place much more difficult.

<u>The Bare Minimum</u> - Some businesses don't have the capital to invest in a state-of-the-art surveillance and monitoring system. Less than reputable businesses may cut corners and only install fewer cameras than what is needed. Even worse, they'll install fake cameras in order to create the appearance of security monitoring. Others will have cameras, but fail to have a recording system or only require the recording system to be operating during business hours.

<u>Mother Nature</u> - Weather can wreck havoc on any mechanical or electrical system. CCTV cameras are not immune despite efforts to protect them with weatherproof housings. Heavy thunderstorms that produce lightning and high winds can render a CCTV camera useless. Even with a sunshade, rain can be driven by the wind onto the lens, obscuring the view.

<u>Vandalism</u> - In an effort to avoid detection or identification, some criminals will vandalize security cameras. Older models are prone to more abuse because of their size. A larger camera is easier to hit with projectile objects in order to render it inoperable or disrupt/alter the desired field of view.

ACTION - Action and movement are what captures the attention of passersby and others in the area. You cannot remain passive in a violent encounter. You must move, choosing to flee or fight. The eyes are drawn to movement. The faster and bigger the movement is, the easier it is to see. In order to get the attention of others, it may be necessary to alert them by getting their ears involved.

I sometimes interchange the word audience for action, as the purpose of the spectator concept is to generate and maintain an audience during a crisis situation, and hopefully inspire or persuade someone to come to your aid.

CAN I HAVE YOUR ATTENTION PLEASE?

In a crisis situation, help is more important than people standing around watching the events unfold. However, no help can be offered if there are no spectators to recruit into assisting. Photo courtesy of www.pixabay.com.

Sprinting - Rapid movement often captures people's attention, provided they're not staring at their Smartphone.

Shouting - Raising your voice brings attention to your situation, especially in places where loud or boisterous conversation is considered rude or socially unacceptable.

Screaming - Nothing gets the attention of a parent like the sound of a screaming child. Unlike shouting, screaming can only be sustained for a short period.

Sobbing - Flowing tears are another method to invoke help. This often works so well at getting someone's attention that criminals use it.

None of the above-mentioned actions may seem indicative of machismo or courageousness and they aren't correlated or reliant on them. Only society in its attempts to use labeling as an indicator and influencer of behavior, suggests that these actions are exclusively held and used by a specific gender or whatever virtue-signaling characteristic is currently fashionable in the eyes of society. The purpose of these techniques is to attract the attention of others, nothing more.

A FINAL WORD...

SERENDIPITY

If *spectators* are the wildcard in this whole equation of Situational Sense, then serendipity is the lottery winner. Serendipity, for the uninitiated, means the occurrence and development of events by chance that produces a beneficial or advantageous outcome. Don't bet on it; don't rely on it. Don't demand or expect it. It's okay to accept it if it comes along, but it is far from a logical back-up plan. Waiting for it will get you hurt or killed. Lucky breaks are often the result of an opponent's incompetence, poor training, or lack of preparedness. Be prepared with competent training and let the perpetrator depend on luck.

The S's of Situational Sense. Graphic by author.

APPENDIX

The following pages contain pictures or diagrams of some of the typical establishments you may encounter during your daily routine. Some of the photos you may encounter while on vacation or visiting larger venues. They serve as examples so that you may conduct your own independent evaluations of other places you frequent. Examine the layouts and ask yourself the corresponding questions:

IMPORTANT NOTE: These are not all inclusive or all encompassing questions, but they give you an idea of the types of questions you should be asking.

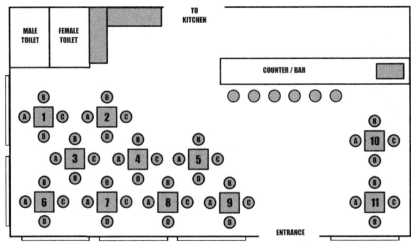

A typical coffee house or bar floor plan. What type of threats could you reasonably expect? Diagram by author.

Where do I normally sit?

Where are the nearest exit(s)?

What area(s) or items offer the best ballistic cover?

What table(s)/chair(s) offers the quickest path of egress?

If I can't exit, what are my other options?

Which table(s)/chair(s) offer the best view of entrances and exits?

Which locations are best for launching a counter-attack with a firearm? With empty hands? With an improvised weapons?

Do the restroom doors lock?

Would I consider causing major property damage (i.e. breaking windows, overturning tables, etc.) to defend myself and/or aid my escape?

Does the establishment have a pro-carry (open or concealed) weapons policy or strict anti-firearm policy?

If no firearms are allowed, does the establishment consent to incur all financial costs and liabilities for ANY type of injury sustained during the commission of a crime on the premises?

What other questions could you ask?

_____

_____

_____

_____

_____

_____

_____

_____

_____

_____

_____

_____

_____

_____

_____

_____

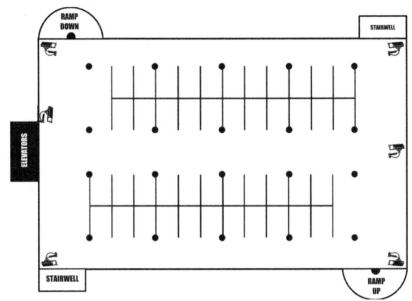

A basic diagram of a multi-level parking lot. What type of threats could you reasonably expect? Diagram by author.

Is parking open to the public or is it a private/corporate lot?

If corporate, are the parking spaces assigned and can you request an available space?

How many levels are present?

Do the support columns (black dots) provide adequate cover?

Are all of the CCTV cameras operational?

Are the cameras static and stationary or do they have pan-tilt-zoom capabilities?

Are there any blind spots where the cameras cannot see?

How much ambient noise is present?

154

Are all the levels well lit?

Do stairwells have proper lighting?

Are there mirrors located in the corners or on support columns?

What other questions could you ask?

_____

_____

_____

_____

_____

_____

_____

_____

_____

_____

_____

_____

_____

_____

_____

What types of threats could you reasonable expect at a park? Photo courtesy of www.unsplash.com

How many exits are present?

Are the pathways sufficiently illuminated?

Does security or police officers patrol the park?

Do locals, tourists, or both frequent the park?

Is the park situated in a commercial or residential area?

Are there any crime statistics available for the area?

Are misdemeanor crimes such as vagrancy, panhandling, and public intoxication a common occurrence here?

Do trees, fences, or other structures obstruct direct paths of travel in the event of an emergency?

Are there any CCTV cameras at major entry/exit points or center display?

Is there music or other performances occurring designed to attract an audience?

Does the park have any major tourist, historical significance, or iconic landmark making it a potential target for terrorist attacks or civil unrest?

What other questions could you ask?

_____

_____

_____

_____

_____

_____

_____

_____

_____

_____

_____

_____

_____

_____

_____

_____

Large stadium venues present a much greater logistical obstacle in navigating
exits and entry points. Photo courtesy of www.unsplash.com

How much time on average does it take to clear the entire venue?

How many exits are available per level?

Where are any potential bottlenecks or choke points?

Where do security personnel attempt to funnel patrons during an
emergency?

Are there roving security teams or hospitality personnel available?

How well do I respond to large, diverse groups of people?

Am I planning to consume alcohol or attend with others within my
group than will consume various amounts of alcohol?

Am I a supporter of the home or opposing team?

What am I choosing to wear and will those choices have the potential to create conflict with other spectators?

Do I intend to use restrooms or concessions during peak times?

What types of EDC equipment will be allowed inside the complex?

Is the venue hosting a high-profile event, which could be targeted by terrorists or protests, i.e. championship games, political rallies, polarizing/controversial public figures?

What other questions could you ask?

_____

_____

_____

_____

_____

_____

_____

_____

_____

_____

_____

_____

_____

YOUR DAILY COMMUTE AND LOCATIONS

You may use the space provided below to write down specific places you frequent and assess them similarly to the previous examples.

_____

_____

_____

_____

_____

_____

_____

_____

_____

_____

_____

_____

_____

_____

_____

_____

HELPFUL ADVICE

1. Study your daily activities. Determine where and when you are most vulnerable and make the necessary changes in your routine.

2. Make a travel cheat sheet. Include the nearest hospitals, police stations, hotels, consulate, tourist traps, and "no-go" zones wherever and whenever you travel. List the names, addresses, telephone numbers, opening hours, after hours/emergency numbers, etc. Research taxi companies or verify availability of ride providers such as Uber, Lyft, Ola, etc. Make one for your city, as well.

3. Learn to become efficient and competent in both armed and unarmed combative systems. Ensure the chosen system trains in combative techniques and tactics; not sport.

4. Keep physically fit. It will help regardless of your choice for fight or flight.

5. Read books, magazine articles, blogs, news stories, etc. relating to situational sense, training, preparedness, and anything else you think will help you prepare.

6. Practice the techniques. Adapt them while sitting, standing, walking, eating, etc. Force yourself to practice in low light/no light, confined spaces, and uncomfortable positions.

7. Limit your distractions. Avoid being sucked into the digital world of technology dependence and distraction.

8. Look up and listen up. Your senses are there to assist you in navigating and analyzing the world around you.

9. There are not points for second place. Ranking and points occur only in sports, not combat and survival.

10. Rules are meant to be broken in a violent confrontation. An attacker (or attackers) has already decided to ignore the rule of law, the rules of engagement, and the rules of manners and etiquette.

11. Do whatever it takes for however long it takes to escape or neutralize the threat in order to stay alive.

12. Avoid drugs and alcohol. This should be a no-brainer when considering illicit/illegal drugs. Prescription medications, over-the-counter remedies, and alcohol can dull your senses, cause drowsiness, and impair your judgment.

13. Get plenty of sleep and eat a balanced diet. Both will help in maintaining the necessary mental focus and alertness needed as you go about your daily routine.

14. Choose your friends and associates carefully. Building trust and knowing that those within your circle of trust have the integrity to watch your back when out together.

15. Assume no one is coming to save you. This reinforces the notion that YOU are responsible for your actions and your safety.

16. Start with training; adding knowledge and more training. Follow that up with routine training and then finalize your training regimen with habitual training.

17. Reread number 16 again and never stop training.

18. Familiarize yourself with the building layouts of the places you frequent the most. Locate as many exits and points of entry when visiting other buildings and venues.

19. If possible, do not frequent or patronage any establishment that openly prohibits or forbids you from defending yourself or protecting others in a manner that is the most beneficial and tactically advantageous to you.

20. Demand that your representatives, elected officials, and civil servants strictly adhere to the oath they've sworn to support and defend the Constitution. Their job is to ensure your rights are never taken away. Anyone in office who does otherwise is a tyrant, traitor, or both.

21. Use backpacks and shoulder bags in order to keep your hands free. Keep one arm free, preferably your dominant arm. If you need to carry something, use your weaker arm.

22. Do not cross your arms, interlace your fingers, place your hands behind your back or on your hips when confronted by potential attackers (or even the police, for that matter).

23. Carry any legally permissible weapon you can and become proficient with its use. Be prepared for the consequences associated with carrying any prohibited items.

24. Choose function over fashion with footwear and apparel choices whenever possible. Avoid footwear that makes running difficult or dangerous. Footwear should be comfortable if you need to walk for long periods.

25. Avoid traveling alone. Use the buddy system when jogging or when walking to your car. Leave in groups when leaving entertainment venues and restaurants.

26. Carry an emergency contact list in your pocket or wallet in case your phone is stolen, damaged, or uncharged. This list should include spouse's phone, children's phone (if applicable) doctor's phone, insurance agent phone, next of kin, attorney phone, US consulate (if overseas), police non-emergency number, bank and credit card company fraud hotline/24-hour customer service numbers, friends or relatives where you're staying.

27. Use every flat, reflective surface to your advantage when looking behind you and extending your peripheral vision. Your mobile phone screen (when darkened) works well, with most people believing you're taking a picture or a selfie.

28. Make detailed travel plans to share with family members and those within your travel party. Set up designated meet-ups and strictly adhere to them. If a meet-up time or location changes, notify everyone concerned.

29. Carry and maintain your EDC (Every Day Carry) kit. Rotate ammunition for firearms, change batteries, check expiration dates on first-aid and trauma kits, and replace any worn out or damaged items.

30. Utilize Gray Man tactics to avoid drawing unwanted attention to yourself, creating excess stimuli, and becoming a potential target to ambushes, assaults, and abductions.

ADDITIONAL RESOURCES

Ball, Philip, *Active Shooter Survival Manual*, 2016, CreateSpace Independent Publishing Platform

Blair, John P., Nichols, Terry, Burns, David, Curnutt, John, *Active Shooter Events and Response*, 2013, CRC Press

Burrese, Alan, *Survive A Shooting: Strategies to Survive Active Shooters and Terrorist attacks*, 2018, TGW Books

Cameron, James CPP, *Active Shooter - Workplace Violence Preparedness: P.A.C.E. Prepare, Act, Care, Evacuate*, 2019, Security Concepts Group, LLC

Cooper, Jeff, *Principles of Personal Defense*, 1972 & 1989, Paladin Press

Dermody, Matthew, *Gray Man: Camouflage for Crowds, Cities, and Civil Crisis*, 2017, CreateSpace Independent Publishing Platform

David, R. and Gray, G., *Risk: A Practical Guide for Deciding What's Really Dangerous in the World Around You,* 2002, Houghton Mifflin Company

Emerson, Clint with Walters, Lynn, *Escape the Wolf: Preemptive Personal Security Handbook* e-book, 2012, Escape the Wolf

Freeborn, Varg, *Violence of Mind: Training and Preparation for Extreme Violence*, 2018, One Life Defense Publishing

Gilliam, Jonathan T., *Sheep No More: The Art of Awareness and Attack Survival*, 2017, Post Hill Press

Hanson, Jason, *Spy Secrets That Can Save Your Life: A Former CIA Officer Reveals Safety and Survival Techniques to Keep You and Your Family Protected*, 2016, Tarcher Perigee

Jannetti, Aaron, *How to Survive an Active Killer: An Honest Look at Your Role in the Age of Mass Violence*, 2017, CreateSpace Independent Publishing Platform

Kardian, Steve, Pistek, A. Clara, *The New Superpower for Women: Trust Your Intuition, Predict Dangerous Situations, and Defend Yourself from the Unthinkable*, 2017, Touchstone

Larkin, Tim, *Survive the Unthinkable: A Total Guide to Women's Self-Protection*, 2013, Rodale Books

Miller, Rory, *Facing Violence: Preparing for the Unexpected*, 2011, YMAA Publication Center

Schneider, Gavriel, *Can I See Your Hands: A Guide to Situational Awareness, Personal Risk Management, Resilience and Security*, 2017, Universal Publishers

Shaffer, Greg, *Stay Safe: Security Secrets for Today's Dangerous World*, 2019, Clovercroft Publishing

Williams, Greg, Scott-Donelan, David, *Combat Observation and Decision-Making in Irregular and Ambiguous Conflicts (CODIAC)*, July 2010

WEBSITE RESOURCES

https://www.personalsafetygroup.com/about/situational-awareness-training/

https://thepreppingguide.com/situational-awareness/

https://en.wikipedia.org/wiki/Situation_awareness

https://worldview.stratfor.com/article/practical-guide-situational-awareness

https://www.artofmanliness.com/articles/10-tests-exercises-and-games-to-heighten-your-senses-and-situational-awareness/

https://tacticalhyve.com/14-ways-to-improve-your-situational-awareness/

https://www.itstactical.com/intellicom/mindset/3-effective-techniques-to-train-your-situational-awareness-and-recognize-change/

https://www.nap.edu/read/6173/chapter/9

https://www.asecurelife.com/situational-awareness-training/

https://sheepdogresponse.com/developing-situational-awareness/

https://securityadviser.net/situational-awareness-exercises/

https://soflete.com/blogs/knowledge/why-situational-awareness-is-the-best-fashion-statement

https://www.addictioncenter.com/drugs/drug-street-names/

https://www.smartertravel.com/10-things-never-wear-traveling-abroad/

https://indianajo.com/how-to-plan-a-trip-planning-an-itinerary.html

https://www.themandagies.com/10-road-trip-planner-tools-apps/

https://travel.state.gov/content/travel/en/traveladvisories/traveladvisories.html/

https://travel.state.gov/content/travel/en/international-travel.html

https://www.dhs.gov/national-terrorism-advisory-system

https://www.protectyourhome.com/home-security-tips

https://home.howstuffworks.com/home-improvement/household-safety/home-security-tips.htm

https://reolink.com/top-diy-home-security-tips-and-tricks/

https://www.ready.gov/active-shooter

TRAINING WEBSITES

Gunsite Academy
2900 W. Gunsite Rd.
Paulden, AZ 86334
928-636-4565
www.gunsite.com

Spearpoint Training Group
1701 S. Main St. #2758
Broken Arrow, OK 74013
539-302-2199
connect@sptraininggroup.com
www.sptraininggroup.com

Scott-Donelan Tracking School (David Scott-Donelan)
3044 Player Avenue
Sierra Vista, AZ 85650
702-498-6765
mantrack@aol.com
www.scottdonelantrackingschool.com

RED - Recognize and Escape Danger
Europe/Africa: +33 6 3041 8844
Asia Pacific/Middle East: +65 6534 5254
contact@redgroup.world
www.redgroup.world

OnPoint Tactical (Kevin Reeve)
St. George, Utah, United States
609-668-5384
info@onpointtactical.com
www.onpointtactical.com

ShivWorks - (Craig Douglas)
www.shivworks.com

Ed's Manifesto - (Ed Calderon)
edsmanifesto@gmail.com
www.edsmanifesto.com

Sheepdog Response - (Tim Kennedy)
PO Box 204116
Austin, TX 78720
512-993-2999
info@sheepdogresponse.com
www.sheepdogresponse.com

Situational Awareness Matters
Gasaway Consulting Group, LLC
1769 Lexington Avenue North
Suite 177
St. Paul, MN 55113-6522
612-548-4424
Support@RichGasaway.com
www.samatters.com

American Survival Co. (Matthew Tate/Aaron Kimball)
Arkansas Base Camp
19436 Crossman Place Road
Hindsville, AR 72738
314-308-6955 (Main office 984-377-2592
americansurvivalschool@gmail.com
www.americansurvivalco.com

Active Response Training
www.activeresponsetraining.net

Self-Preservation Training, LLC
9675 E. 148th St. #200
Noblesville, IN 46060
317-379-4730
selfpreservationtraining@gmail.com
www.selfpreservationtraining.com

The Diamond Arrow Group * (Kelly Sayre)
info@thediamondarrowgroup.com
www.thediamondarrowgroup.com

* NOTE: This organization addresses the specific needs and concerns of female clients.

Battleline Tactical (Kris Paronto w/ Christopher Doner)
www.battlelinetactical.net

ABOUT THE AUTHOR

Matthew Dermody is the author of six other books about camouflage/concealment and urban survival. He has a degree in Criminal Justice, with nearly 20 years of experience working in various facets of the security industry in both the United States and Australia. He currently resides in Perth, Australia with his wife and their twin girls.

Printed in Great Britain
by Amazon

74980525R00108